ECLIPSE OF DREAMS

THE UNDOCUMENTED-LED STRUGGLE FOR FREEDOM

ECLIPSE OF DREAMS

THE UNDOCUMENTED-LED STRUGGLE FOR FREEDOM

EDITED BY PEDRO SANTIAGO MARTINEZ, CLAUDIA MUÑOZ, MARIELA NUÑEZ-JANES, STEPHEN PAVEY, FIDEL CASTRO RODRIGUEZ, MARCO SAAVEDRA

AK PRESS

Eclipse of Dreams: The Undocumented-Led Struggle for Freedom

© 2020 Pedro Santiago Martinez Claudia Muñoz, Mariela Nuñez-Janes, Stephen Pavey, Fidel Castro Rodriguez, and Marco Saavedra
This edition © 2020 AK Press

ISBN: 978-1-84935-381-6
E-ISBN: 978-1-84935-382-3
Library of Congress Control Number: 2019947443

AK Press   AK Press
370 Ryan Ave. #100   33 Tower St.
Chico, CA 95973   Edinburgh EH6 7BN
United States   Scotland
www.akpress.org   www.akuk.com
akpress@akpress.org   ak@akedin.demon.co.uk

The above addresses would be delighted to provide you with the latest AK Press distribution catalog, which features books, pamphlets, zines, and stylish apparel published and/or distributed by AK Press. Alternatively, visit our websites for the complete catalog, latest news, and secure ordering.

Printed in the United States

CONTENTS

Prelude   1

Introduction   11

Chapter 1: Shadows then Light   31

Chapter 2: The Mis-Education of the Migrant   69

Chapter 3: A Deported DREAMer's Story   85

Chapter 4: Layers of Pain   101

Chapter 5: Brothers Crossing Borders   121

Chapter 6: Acompañando   135

Image Captions for Photos   145

Prelude

"One discovers the light in darkness, that is what darkness is for; but everything in our lives depends on how we bear the light. It is necessary, while in darkness, to know that there is a light somewhere, to know that in oneself, waiting to be found, there is a light. What the light reveals is danger, and what it demands is faith."
—James Baldwin, *Nothing Personal*

"Ahogadas, escupimos el oscuro.
Peleando con nuestra propia sombra
El silencio nos sepulta."

"Drowning, spitting the dark.
Fighting with our own shadows
The silence buries us."
—Gloria Anzaldúa, *Borderlands / La Frontera*

Some things can only be learned in the darkness. We had already come to realize this somewhere deep within our bodies, from sharing our stories and listening to those of so many other courageous youth coming out of the shadows, declaring, "I am undocumented and unafraid."[1] What we had come to know as true, we learned by navigating

1. Stephen Pavey, "Out of the Shadows and Into the Light: Undocumented, Unashamed, and Unafraid—A New Immigrant Movement Builds Momentum," *PRISM* (May/June, 2011): 28-34.

the contradictions lived deep within experiences of illegality, inequality, and the everyday threat of deportability. Our common struggle for human freedom, and at times simply for survival, led to that moment in 2010, imbued with optimism, hard work, and determination—that moment where belonging, civil rights, upward mobility, and a path to citizenship seemed possible. This was our dream.

On December 18, 2010, the Senate gallery of the U.S. Capitol could scarcely hold the multitude of undocumented youth, family, and friends. It was crowded with hope. Some of us woke early that morning to brave the harsh cold, the long lines passing through the Capitol's visitor center security. Most importantly, we braved the Senate vote on the DREAM Act (Development, Relief, and Education for Alien Minors). Others gathered across the U.S. in living rooms, classrooms, and community halls, sitting in front of televisions tuned in to the Senate vote streaming live on C-Span. Some waited and watched alone.

What was this DREAM that we were all waiting for? The "DREAM Act" is the name given to a series of proposed legislative Acts that, since first introduced in 2001, promised to provide an estimated 2.1 million undocumented 1.5-generation youth in the United States, a path toward legal status.[2] The terms of eligibility changed over the years since its introduction in 2001, but in general, one would need to provide evidence of entering the country under the age of sixteen, have lived in the U.S. for at least five years, graduated from high school, demonstrate good moral character, and commit either to a path toward college education or service in the military.

What was about to happen in the Senate Gallery was important because it represented a struggle of almost a decade. To put our concerns and dreams into perspective, nearly 65,000 undocumented youth graduate from American high schools each year. This undocumented 1.5-generation—born outside the U.S. but raised in it—is

---

2. Jeanne Batalova and Margie McHugh, "DREAM vs. Reality: An Analysis of Potential DREAM Act Beneficiaries," (Migration Policy Institute, 2010), http://www.migrationpolicy.org/research/dream-vs-reality-analysis-potential-dream-act-beneficiaries.

caught in a legal paradox. Although guaranteed free public primary and secondary education by the Supreme Court decision *Plyler v. Doe* in 1982, these students today face the contradictions of limited opportunities for college education and social mobility.[3] After high school, those who do finish must contend with limited access to financial aid, out of state tuition rates (except in seventeen states), the inability to work legally, and a host of restrictions on their movement and rights in the country that most refer to as "home."

Unfortunately, only an estimated five to ten percent pursue higher education.[4] Many never graduate from high school and the majority chooses to work at low-wage jobs because of the social, institutional, legal, and financial barriers they face.[5] There is an increasing awareness of the mental health issues, such as depression and suicide, among undocumented youth. The tragic case of Joaquin Luna, an undocumented Texas student, whose suicide made national headlines in 2011, is a case in point. Joaquin's dream was to become a civil engineer. Unable to cope with the limitations of their status, youth like Joaquin "find themselves ill-prepared for the mismatch between their levels of education and the limited options that await them in the low-wage, clandestine labor market."[6] While much of the national research and media attention focus on the small percentage of highly successful undocumented youth, also known

3. Michael A. Olivas, *No Undocumented Child Left Behind: Plyler v. Doe and the Education of Undocumented Schoolchildren* (New York: NYU Press, 2012); Rubén G. Rumbaut, "Ages, Life Stages, and Generational Cohorts: Decomposing the Immigrant First and Second Generations in the United States," *International Migration Review* 38, no. 3 (2004): 1160–1205; Hinda Seif, "The Civic Education and Engagement of Latina/o Immigrant Youth: Challenging Boundaries and Creating Safe Spaces," (Woodrow Wilson International Center for Scholars, 2009), https://www.wilsoncenter.org/sites/default/files/Seif%20-%20Challenging%20Boundaries%20and%20Creating%20Safe%20Spaces.pdf.

4. Roberto G. Gonzales, "Wasted Talent and Broken Dreams: The Lost Potential of Undocumented Students," *In Focus* 5, no. 13 (2007): 1–11.

5. Roberto G. Gonzales, "Learning to be Illegal: Undocumented Youth and Shifting Legal Contexts in the Transition to Adulthood," *American Sociological Review* 76, no. 4 (2011): 602–19; Ryan Evely Gildersleeve, "Access Between and Beyond Borders," *Journal of College Admission*, issue 206 (Winter 2010): 3–10.

6. Gonzales, "Learning to be Illegal," 616.

as "DREAMers," it is important to recognize the vast majority remain in the shadows. They, along with the larger undocumented community, face the very real possibility of joining a permanent underclass.[7]

Some estimate that nearly 20,000 undocumented youth were mobilized to action during the year leading up to the possible passage of the DREAM Act. The year 2009 closed with a successful public campaign led by undocumented youth in Chicago to end the deportation of a student attending the University of Illinois at Chicago. Many saw 2010 as the year for the DREAM Act to come true. Four undocumented youth set off on January 1, 2010, from Florida on the "trail of dreams," a walk of 1,500 miles to Washington, D.C. The first public coming out event as "undocumented and unafraid" was held in March in front of Immigration and Custom Enforcement (ICE) offices in Chicago. The "trail of dreams" ended in D.C. in May with a press conference where thirty-five immigrant rights advocates were arrested. Just a few weeks later, five undocumented youth engaged in civil disobedience with a sit-in at Senator John McCain's office in Phoenix and were arrested on the anniversary of *Brown vs. Board of Education*. Throughout the summer, undocumented youth continued mobilizing. In Texas, Kentucky, Michigan, New York, North Carolina, and California there were hunger strikes. In July, undocumented youth traveled across the country to Washington D.C. for the DREAM University Graduation, the largest mock graduation of undocumented students to date, and following the demonstration twenty-one undocumented youth were arrested for civil disobedience. Across the country undocumented youth on college campuses were organizing DREAM teach-ins, phone banks, lobbying efforts, prayer vigils, and even more hunger strikes. In September, the DREAM Act failed to pass as an amendment that was attached to a Department

7.   Leisy J. Abrego, "I Can't Go to College Because I Don't Have Papers: Incorporation Patterns of Undocumented Latino Youth," *Latino Studies* 4, no. 3 (Autumn 2006): 212–23; Gonzales, "Learning to be Illegal"; Carola Suarez-Orozco, Robert T. Teranishi, Hirokazu Yoshikawa, and Marcelo Suárez-Orozco, "Growing Up in the Shadows: The Developmental Implications of Unauthorized Status," *Harvard Educational Review* 81, no. 3 (September 2011): 438–73.

of Defense authorization bill. Behind the scenes, politicians debated the timeliness of a stand-alone DREAM Act versus a push for comprehensive immigration reform.

Waiting until the very last weeks of the legislative season, politicians decided to push for the DREAM Act as a stand-alone bill during the lame duck session, a name that did not portend good news for our efforts. In early December, hundreds of undocumented youth across the country quit jobs and left final papers and exams to come to D.C. to organize for the DREAM Act. We worked nearly around the clock lobbying and organizing. On one day alone, we organized an effort of 77,000 phone calls supporting the DREAM Act. There were more prayer vigils and hunger strikes. There was Christmas caroling through the halls of Congress, with lyrics revised to support the DREAM Act, "Oh, senators, oh senators, please pass the DREAM Act now." We organized a DREAM blood drive, a DREAM Sabbath, DREAM homework sit-ins in the congressional cafeterias, and a reenactment of the march around Jericho, now the Capitol, praying that the walls standing against the DREAM Act would fall. And all of this hard work and determination paid off with the passage of the DREAM Act in the House of Representatives on December 8, 2010. Now all that was needed was for the Senate to pass this version and the President to sign it.

The morning for this important vote on the DREAM finally came. By 9:00 a.m. the Senate gallery was largely full. The Senate was called to order and then a prayer was offered for wisdom for our legislators, that they would be "turned away from false solutions."[8] Two hours passed as senators took turns speaking to either the DREAM Act or the Don't Ask, Don't Tell Repeal Act. We listened to people with fears of illegals crossing our borders, calling this bill "amnesty" and a reward for criminal behavior. Others pleaded on behalf of the DREAMers, explaining that it was through "no fault of their own" that they were in the U.S. without papers. As we heard the voices of supposed support some of us cringed in our seats. If the DREAMers were not at fault, then who

---

8.   "Senate Session," *C-SPAN* (December 18, 2010), http://www.c-span.org/video/?297168-1/senate-session.

is to blame? Our parents? The case for the DREAM Act was made by painting a picture of DREAMers as model citizens deserving of a path toward legalization. Supporters described DREAMers' potential to add to the U.S. economy through their hard work. They said that DREAMers "played by the rules and only want to achieve the American Dream." Senator Durbin pointed to the Senate gallery and made a case for the DREAM Act by telling those present, look, "they are valedictorians, captains of teams, leaders of their communities ... possessing high GPAs, sciences degrees ... why would you deny them a chance to make America a better place?"[9]

Two and a half hours after the Senate was called to order, at 11:31 a.m., the chair reminded the gallery that "expressions of approval or disapproval are not permitted." Around the gallery we all held each other's hands. The fate of the DREAM Act, our fate, was clear as we watched each Senator come forward to cast their vote, some very visibly with their thumbs down. "The motion is not agreed to." The DREAM Act died, just five votes short of the sixty needed to advance the bill.

It was so close. There was a visible numbness among us, a shock that immediately gave way to tears and strong embraces across the gallery. What now—now that we witnessed this eclipse of dreams?

Some of us were physically present at the senate gallery other of us watched from afar. Together we experienced the euphoria of possibilities and the despair of disappointment.

Fighting with Our Own Shadows: Journeys of Faith

In other places and times, an eclipse warned of imminent danger, disaster, even the end of the world. The failure of the DREAM Act felt like this. Yet in the darkness of this moment, it did not take long to see a glimpse of light. Maybe, just maybe, the eclipse was a warning to us. What if our dreams, the very scope of our horizons, what we hoped

---

9. Ibid.

for ourselves and others, was limited by the framework in which we expressed them, the American Dream itself? What if, out of our real pain and desire for freedom, we had become pawns in a system where freedom is an illusion? Did we lose track of our ends and compromise our means because of this dream framework? What if United We Dream and the political-economic power behind those that claimed to represent us under a united dream were never united and confused dreams with lies? What if, from the outset, our framing of the issue, our struggle for freedom was itself problematic? In the darkness, we began to realize that the search for a solution to the immigration problem, when mired in the rationale of the American Dream, was part of the problem.

As we asked ourselves these questions and contemplated the end of our world, the end of the dream, we began to follow the light that we had found in our own lives and the love within our community and shared struggle for freedom. We began to understand the lives and choices of our parents as filled with dignity and courage. Instead of blaming them, we praised them for their faith to risk everything for their children. And now that darkness eclipsed our personal dreams, we saw the absurdity of what W.E.B. Du Bois described as the "strong man," the DREAMer, "fighting to be free in order that another people should not be free."[10] We were beginning to see that the dream for collective freedom and the dignity of all humanity was not only a greater dream but one in conflict with the American Dream.

What passed as an eclipse was possibly a reminder that what was lost, had it been won, might have truly destroyed us. We might have won our access to the American Dream, at the expense of the greater struggle for our freedom. "Uncle" Vincent Harding would later tell us that it was lazy journalists and historians who had framed what was a Black-led struggle for freedom as a "civil rights" movement, attempting to squeeze something vast into a legislative straitjacket.[11] Similarly, Michelle Alexander challenged

---

10. W.E.B. Du Bois, *The Autobiography of W.E.B. Du Bois: A Soliloquy on Viewing My Life from the Last Decade of Its First Century* (New York: International Publishers, 1968), 146.

11. Stephen Pavey, "The Immigration Industrial Complex: America, You Must be Born Again," *PRISM*

us to consider what was lost, when we celebrated the granting of certain civil rights by embracing a politics of respectability.[12]

We were reminded of what we were learning in the dark when President Barack Obama spoke to the nation just a month after the DREAM Act's defeat, saying, "Today, there are hundreds of thousands of students excelling in our schools who are not American citizens. Some are the children of undocumented workers, who had nothing to do with the actions of their parents ... as soon as they obtain advanced degrees, we send them back home to compete against us. It makes no sense ... let's stop expelling talented, responsible young people who could be staffing our research labs or starting a new business, who could be further enriching this nation."[13]

For the "strong man," the perfect Dreamer, to gain rights meant that the bad Dreamer was deportable and, further, that the "illegal" dreams of the perfect Dreamer's parents were worthless. We began to see that the criteria for the DREAM Act re-inscribed and re-enforced race and class barriers to inclusion in this society. The DREAM Act would bar the rest of the undocumented community from becoming free. The American Dream came with great costs.

We continue to search for light and discover hope in the darkness. James Baldwin may best describe what we learned: "Any real change implies the breakup of the world as one has always known it, the loss of all that gave one an identity, the end of safety. Yet, it is only when a man is able, without bitterness or self-pity, to surrender a dream he has long cherished or a privilege he has long possessed that he is set free—he has set himself free—for higher dreams, for greater privileges."[14] This greater privilege is the

(March/April 2013): 8–16.

12. Michelle Alexander, *The New Jim Crow: Mass Incarceration in the Age of Colorblindness* (New York: The New Press, 2012).

13. Barack Obama, "Remarks by the President in State of Union Address," transcript, https://www.whitehouse.gov/the-press-office/2011/01/25/remarks-president-state-union-address.

14. James Baldwin, *The Price of a Ticket: Collected Nonfiction 1948–1985* (New York: St. Martin's Press, 1985), 147.

struggle for our *collective* freedom, for our *collective* humanity, for our *collective* dignity. Du Bois warned us that the great tragedy of our time for undocumented families, for this nation and the world, is not poverty, wickedness, or ignorance, but that humans know so little of humanity.[15]

In the next pages, we invite you to learn about our journeys through the darkness as we search for light after the eclipse of dreams; to learn, through our stories of struggle and fear, of living "illegal," a little more about what it means to be human, to discover dignity, and what it might mean to shed light on our global humanity.

15. "Men know so little of men" in his phrasing. W.E.B. Du Bois, *The Souls of Black Folk* (New York: Oxford University Press, 2007), 152.

Introduction

"De tal manera que el mundo hispánico no vino a los Estados Unidos, sino que los Estados Unidos vinieron al mundo hispánico. Quizás sea un acto de equilibrio y aun de justicia poética que hoy el mundo hispánico regrese tanto a los Estados Unidos como a una parte a veces olvidada de su herencia ancestral en el hemisferio americano."

"In this way the Hispanic world did not return to the U.S., instead the U.S. returned to the Hispanic world. Perhaps it is an act of equilibrium or even poetic justice that today the Hispanic world returns so much to the United States like a forgotten part of its ancestral heritage in the American Hemisphere."
　　—Carlos Fuentes, *El Espejo Enterrado*

There are six of us who came together to write and edit this book collectively. Five of us are not U.S. citizens. Four of us have experienced an "undocumented" status. Two of us have PhDs. We met each other somewhere in between classrooms, academic conferences, and organizing for the DREAM Act. Our collective story begins in 2010 in the chambers of Congress where U.S. justice pretends to reside and freedom is said to be protected by rule of law. We can trace all of our relationships back to that year of organizing and education. The lived experiences of the main protagonists of our collective story—Marco, Clau, Pedro, Fidel, and Shaun—cast a shadow on the values and story told of the U.S. as an exceptional beacon of democracy and hope. Our testimonials take us through distant times and places while simultaneously placing us in the present as they intertwine with the politics of immigration and practices of liberation. The lives of Marco, Clau, Pedro, Fidel, and Shaun reflect the ways that the U.S. and Latin America have been connected over time, and reveal a kind of poetic justice, as Carlos Fuentes puts it, when the movement of peoples from South to North is viewed through the eyes of those who make this daring journey. By following our journeys across multiple borders, we invite you into the contradictory spaces inhabited by four undocumented youth as we seek freedom and navigate deeply rooted terrains of injustice. We discuss the forces that pushed and pulled us toward and away from the mythos of the American Dream, and we interrogate the role of social scientists, particularly anthropologists Mariela and Stephen, who witnessed the collision of dreams and nightmares unfold.

From Border Crossings to Wall Building

Scholars of migration explain movements of people across national boundaries as related to push and pull factors. Push factors refer to the conditions in the home country that propel individuals to migrate. Push factors include economic insecurity, political persecution, fear, and a history of family migration. Pull factors are the conditions in the host country that propel migrants towards a particular destination. Pull factors include jobs, security, family, education. Push factors are often characterized as creating conditions of insecurity, while pull factors promise to provide conditions of security for migrants in their host country.

However, in the context of migration from Latin America to the U.S., conditions are more complex as they are complicated by a legacy of internal colonization and ambivalent reception.[1] In his acclaimed book, *Occupied America*, Rodolfo Acuña argues that

---

1. Wayne A. Cornelius, "Ambivalent Reception: Mass Public Responses to the 'New' Latino Immigration to the United States," in *Latinos Remaking America*, edited by Marcelo M. Suárez-Orozco and Mariela M. Páez. (Berkeley: University of California Press, 2002).

Mexican-Americans are a colonized minority.[2] Their internal colonization stems from a long history of cultural subjugation and conquest. Many Mexican-Americans, including Acuña, claim that the "border crossed us," referring to a forgotten history of conquest of Mexico by the U.S. that led to the appropriation of over half of Mexico's territory and the establishment of the U.S.–Mexico border along the Rio Grande. An understanding of this was evident in many of the signs held by protesters in immigrant protests and walk-outs in recent years since the mass marches of 2006 in protest of HR 4437—The Border Protection, Antiterrorism, and Illegal Immigration Control Act, one of the most draconian pieces of legislation, which aimed to criminalize anyone providing assistance to undocumented immigrants.

The continuing effects of colonization are evident, according to Acuña, in the enduring economic, political, educational marginalization of the U.S.'s Mexican-American population and the suspicion that there is something un-American or anti-American about their Mexican heritage. For example, during the mega-marches and the nationwide demonstrations that followed in 2006, participants were instructed by organizers to bring U.S. flags instead of Mexican flags or flags from their countries of origin. Similarly, in a newspaper article about a 2010 march in support of comprehensive immigration reform, an organizer justified the displays of U.S. flags and white t-shirts explaining that, "If we don't show patriotism, and lead patriotism, how can we be respected as patriots in the country?"[3]

Black scholar and activist, W.E.B. Du Bois also wrote about a legacy of suspicion and questioning of Black allegiance to the U.S., which he termed "double consciousness."[4] According to Du Bois, Black people in the U.S. struggle to reconcile their identity as Africans and Americans, as they continuously "have this sense of always looking at one's

2. Rodolfo Acuña, *Occupied America: A History of Chicanos* (New York: Pearson, 2010).
3. Anna M. Tinsley, "Protesters Will Take to the Streets Saturday in Dallas for Immigration Overhaul," *Star-Telegram*, April 29, 2010.
4. Du Bois, *The Souls of Black Folk*, 8.

self through the eyes of others [white society], of measuring one's soul by the tape of a world that looks on in amused contempt and pity."[5] While there is at the same time this internal struggle against anti-Blackness, there is also the very real struggle of those same forces of contempt and state violence experienced on bodies. Black parents in the U.S. are forced to have "the talk" with their kids, in which they prepare their children for encounters with police. Black parents hope that their message of compliance and politeness in the presence of police officers is enough to convince police to spare their child's life during routine traffic stops. For Blacks and Latinos in the U.S., the struggle to be presumed innocent and treated fairly is an integral part of their American experience.

Michelle Alexander argues that the move from the Jim Crow–era to today, when racial hierarchy can no longer be maintained by using "race" or segregation, involves a shift to questions of "law and order."[6] This strategy of criminalizing and incarcerating the Black community is now being used against the immigrant community, while at the same time new categories of un-deservedness are created. In U.S. immigration law, the Immigration and Naturalization Act of 1965 (INA) is supposedly implemented based on the following principles: reunifying families, admitting immigrants with skills valuable to the economy, protecting refugees, and promoting diversity. INA replaced the system of national quotas based on national origin and race that was in place since the 1920s and drove immigration policy for much of U.S. history. While much of this system was broken and shifting under the Obama administration, we are now seeing, under the Trump administration, even greater shifts in implementation of this immigration law and the creation of new policies incongruent with the law. The principles of the INA are mediated by a 7% annual per country cap and a complex system of allocations of preferences. The significant shift in migration to the U.S. from Latin America in the 1990s prompted the Illegal Immigration Reform and Immigrant Responsibility Act of 1996 (IIRIRA), which contributed to the militarization and

5. Ibid.
6. Alexander, *The New Jim Crow*, 50–51.

criminalization of immigration through efforts of border control (including interior enforcement), penalties against smuggling and document fraud, detention, deportation, and barring deported immigrants from legal entry into the U.S. for ten years. In particular, IIRIRA made almost any criminal offense, regardless of its severity, grounds for immigrant deportation, and created a process of "expedited removal" that granted immigration agents discretion.

IIRIRA gave credibility to public fears about the criminality of immigrants, particularly Latinos. While race and national origin were explicitly erased from policies of inclusion and exclusion, IIRIRA inserted migration into the public discourse of criminality covertly implicating race and national origin in a national policy of persecution and expulsion. The tragic events of 9/11 contributed to solidifying public fears and provided justification to make immigration the interest of national security. In 2003, Immigration and Naturalization Services (INS) moved from the Department of Justice, where it had been located since 1940, to the newly created Department of Homeland Security, its functions separated into three agencies, U.S. Citizenship and Immigration Services (USCIS), Immigration and Customs Enforcement (ICE), and Customs and Border Protection (CBP). The shift from the Department of Justice to Homeland Security in matters related to immigration coincides with a rise in hate crimes targeting Muslims, Latinos, and transgender groups, police brutality against Indigenous peoples, Blacks, and Latinos, and wide-spread incidences of gun violence.

Fighting Illegality

Fast forward to today. The ambivalence of public opinion and policy is still challenged by the certainty of undocumented youth and immigrant organizing. For some time, both immigrant identities and cycles of rebellion were clearly linked to executive and legislative actions. After the U.S. Supreme Court decided to allow a lower court's block on President Obama's 2014 executive order known as DAPA (Deferred Action for Parental Accountability), migrants around the country took to the streets demanding that the president take action to save DAPA in order to extend temporary legal immigration status to millions of undocumented parents in the U.S. The urgency for action was a rallying cry for thousands of migrants in the U.S. and beyond. Following the 2006 student walkouts and historic marches for immigrant rights, undocumented youth began organizing independently or in coalition with other immigrant rights organizations in order to educate local communities about their rights, push state legislators to support bills to allow undocumented students to enroll in universities as in-state students, halt anti-immigrant state measures, and harness national support for the DREAM Act.[7] Undocumented youth in particular adopted the practice of "coming out of the shadows," a strategy of self-disclosure about their status and a justification for their deserving legalization through the DREAM Act. As undocumented youth publicly disclosed their status they also crafted a narrative through which they presented their experiences as American students who happened to be undocumented. They used their experiences in the U.S. school system and their expectation of a college education to emphasize their American ideals and desire for an American Dream. They relied on their forgotten memories of their country of origin and in some cases ignorance about their status to justify the urgency for legislation that would recognize their sense of cultural belonging as deserving of legalization.

In her 2012 discussion of trainings for undocumented youth organizers, Laura Corrunker notes the importance of stories in articulating common experiences.[8] Stories including themes of pursuing the American Dream, working hard, living in fear, and overcoming obstacles were some of the ways that undocumented youth articulated shared experiences and built a movement. Publicly sharing stories became one of the ways that undocumented youth challenged the dehumanizing effects of criminalization

7. The DREAM Act is a U.S. legislative proposal, which has taken many forms over the years since 2001, that would grant legal status to qualifying immigrants who entered the United States as minors.

8. Laura Corrunker, "'Coming Out of the Shadows': Dream Act Activism in the Context of Global Anti-Deportation Activism," *Indiana Journal of Global Legal Studies* 19, no. 1 (2012): 143.

and built public support. For example, at the 2016 Democratic National Convention, Astrid Silva began her speech in support of the nomination of Hillary Clinton by telling the audience,

> When I was four years old, my mother and I climbed into a raft, and we crossed the river to join my father in America in search of a better life. All I had was a little doll. I grew up like an ordinary girl. My dad worked as a landscaper, and my mom stayed at home with my brother and I. But while my friends did ordinary things, I couldn't, because my parents were afraid that someone might discover I was undocumented. My family believed so deeply in the promise of this country that we risked everything for the American Dream.[9]

The emphasis on the American Dream, on pursuing ordinary lives under extraordinary circumstances, in stories like Astrid Silva's, helped build support for the DREAM Act by disrupting the narrative of illegality with the image of the deserving immigrant. The term "illegal" was replaced with "DREAMer." Yet, in the effort to become "ordinary," to live a life deemed worthy of acceptance, the complexities of Astrid Silva's life and the stories of millions of DREAMers were erased, forgotten, made irrelevant. In Astrid's case, as in the case of others, we learned about her heroic efforts at graduating college, how she had benefited from DACA (Deferred Action for Childhood Arrivals, an executive memorandum issued by President Obama in 2012), and then, as an afterthought, we heard about her parents' continuing fear.

The eligibility criteria for DACA and the more recent American Dream and Promise Act, passed by the House of Representatives in 2019, focus on when an immigrant arrived in the U.S. (i.e. as innocent children) and their educational achievement or

---

9. Yara Simon, "7 DNC Speakers Who Stood Up for Immigrants in Day 1's Fiery Speeches," *Remezcla*, July 26, 2016, https://remezcla.com/lists/culture/7-dnc-speakers-who-stood-up-for-immigrants-in-day-1s -fiery-speeches/.

military participation. The undocumented migrants who do not hurdle over those barriers are deemed the "bad illegals" versus the good DREAMers, good citizens. These criteria re-inscribe and re-enforce race and class barriers to inclusion in society, barring the rest of the undocumented community from gaining access to human dignity and civil rights in this country. They also re-enforce xenophobic and racist attitudes and behaviors towards the undocumented population that many American citizens hold and act upon. The undocumented-led movement for freedom we document in this book is a challenge to this narrative of the "good citizen," the good neoliberal subject who embodies the values that keep the myth of the American Dream alive.

Anthropologist Leo Chavez discusses the decision to cross the U.S.–Mexico Border illegally as a "monumental event" in the lives of undocumented immigrants.[10] Certainly, as Chavez recounts in his ethnography of undocumented farmworkers in San Diego, this decision profoundly impacts the lives of migrants. Many die during the dangerous journey. If they survive the crossing, they contend with physical and emotional trauma in addition to complicated legal challenges. Fear shadows every aspect of the ordinary lives of undocumented immigrants. DREAMers like Astrid attempted to disrupt this fear by naming their own experience and disclosing their status. Yet, even for DREAMers like Astrid, the achievement of the American Dream is illusory: it does not completely lift the shadow of fear. In Astrid's case, her parents, who were deemed undeserving of DACA, DAPA, or comprehensive immigration reform, continue to live with the fear of deportation. And with the election of Donald Trump fear returned to young people like Astrid, because the future of DACA has become even more uncertain. "Rights" bestowed by the state can just as easily be taken away by the state. The persecution of migrants in the form of deportations and raids is part of ordinary life for families like Astrid's. The fear of deportation runs so deep among the almost eleven million undocumented immigrants in the U.S., that in 2013, according to the

10. Leo Chavez, *Shadowed Lives: Undocumented Immigrants in American Society* (Belmont: Wadsworth Publishing, 2012), 5.

Pew Research Center, 55 percent of Latinos believed that some kind of relief from the threat of deportation was more important than a pathway to citizenship.[11] Similarly, in 2018, 55 percent of Latinos surveyed by the Pew Research Center worried about deportation.[12] This urgency stems in part from the increasing persecution of immigrants through raids and the systematic targeting of mostly undocumented Latinos in the form of over two million deportations.

This war on immigrants has recently been ramped up. Massive deportation numbers have been a feature of both Democratic and Republican administrations, and they reached unheard of heights under President Obama. However, President Trump has drastically increased attention and resources toward the detention of immigrants, significantly militarizing the southern border and locking up immigrants along the border and in the interior. The truth of the massive incarceration of Latinos is that it includes children fleeing violence, targets Central Americans, and underscores disturbing government relationship with private prison companies. This relationship is fueled by detention quotas and includes violations of human rights and medical care standards. There are 209 immigrant detention facilities in the U.S., according to Detention Watch Network, a national coalition that challenges the detention system, 62 percent of the facilities are operated by private companies. Private oversight makes it extremely difficult for outsiders to access the facilities and makes enforcement of minimum regulations a challenge. These facilities operated from 2009 until 2017 under a bed-quota mandated by the U.S. Congress that requires ICE to maintain 34,000 beds at any given time. This quota system

11. Mark Hugo Lopez, Paul Taylor, Cary Funk, and Ana Gonzalez-Barrera, "On Immigration Policy, Deportation Relief Seen As More Important than Citizenship," Pew Research Center, December 19, 2013, http://www.pewhispanic.org/2013/12/19/on-immigration-policy-deportation-relief-seen-as-more-important-than-citizenship/.

12. Mark Hugo Lopez, Ana Gonzalez-Barrera, and Jens Manuel Krogstad, "More Latinos Have Serious Concerns about their Place in America under Trump," Pew Research Center, October 25, 2019, https://www.pewresearch.org/hispanic/2018/10/25/more-latinos-have-serious-concerns-about-their-place-in-america-under-trump/.

has since been abandoned under the Trump administration, but not to reduce its size. Instead, there are now, in 2019, as many as 54,000 immigrants incarcerated within the U.S. prison system with new for-profit immigrant detentions being built at record pace.

The fear of deportation also affects the daily lives of young U.S. citizens who are part of mixed status families. The majority of children of undocumented parents between 2009 and 2013 were U.S. citizens (79 percent), but they know that citizenship does not safeguard them from persecution.[13] The social as well as psychological consequences are devastating. Families are broken, the foster care system is overwhelmed, and young people are left to navigate the education system on their own.

In great part, the nightmare of detention and deportation was brought to light through the activism and organizing efforts of undocumented youth. In 2013, in an action called the #DREAM9 and #BringThemHome campaign, three "high-profile" undocumented youth activists self-deported and returned to the U.S. through the Nogales Port of Entry, with six other undocumented youth who had been deported under the Obama administration. These DREAMers, wearing their caps and gowns, asked for humanitarian parole and, through their personal experiences, were able to document the unjust realities of detention while organizing within these immigration prisons.

Undocumented migrants experience life at the intersection of dreams and nightmares. Their lives are shadowed by fears and simultaneously sustained by the freedom to name their reality and confront their oppressor. The testimonial narratives in this book focus on the space where these nightmares and dreams intersect, the third space that Chicana feminist scholar Gloria Anzaldúa calls *la encrucijada*/the crossroads. The stories tell us about what is like to live at this intersection and suggest what this vision reveals about the quest for a better life. We call this intersectional space, where shadows meets light, the "Eclipse of Dreams."

---

13. Randy Capps, Michael Fix, and Jie Zong, "A Profile of U.S. Children with Unauthorized Immigrant Parents," Migration Policy Institute Fact Sheet, January 2019, https://www.migrationpolicy.org/research/profile-us-children-unauthorized-immigrant-parents.

Two of the authors of this book, Steve and Mariela, are anthropologists and came to these issues, initially at least, as anthropologists. Through our interactions with undocumented youth activists, we and our work were transformed.

As a discipline with deep colonial roots, anthropology struggles with its close relationship to colonialism. Women and minorities in the discipline have historically remained on the margins or struggled to have their contributions recognized and included in the anthropological canon.[14] Over the history of the discipline, anthropologists of color and non-U.S.-based anthropologists, have contributed a problem-oriented or applied approach to ethnography, pursued dialogical forms of writing, and engaged in activist anthropology.[15] Despite these contributions, the discipline is still resistant to ideas and practices that challenge its colonial core. In particular, it has been difficult for anthropology to engage disciplines that, like ethnic and Chicano studies, emerged from decolonial social movements, incorporate research conducted by Latin American anthropologists, and consider activism a legitimate site of inquiry and knowledge production.[16]

Orisanmi Burton argues that the Black Lives Matter movement, "expose[s] the limitations of ethnographic methodology and disrupt[s] the anthropology of race" because it offers a "powerful political vocabulary" that fills a "critical gap in what is known about state violence in the United States."[17] This movement, as he suggests, calls into question anthropologists' ethnographic authority because organizers and protesters rely, like anthropologists, on their observations, descriptions, and analysis of the criminalization and killings of Blacks by actors sanctioned by the state, not just to understand but also

14. Louise Lamphere, "The Convergence of Applied, Practicing, and Public Anthropology in the 21st Century," *Human Organization* 63, no. 4 (Winter 2004): 431–43.

15. Ibid.

16. Karen Mary Davalos, "Chicano/a Studies and Anthropology: The Dialogue that Never Was," *Aztlán: A Journal of Chicano Studies* 23, no. 2 (October 1998): 13–45.

17. Orisanmi Burton, "Black Lives Matter: A Critique of Anthropology," *Cultural Anthropology* Editors' Forum, June 29, 2015, https://culanth.org/fieldsights/black-lives-matter-a-critique-of-anthropology.

to act. Insurgent research could help acknowledge, according to Burton, that a Black transnational tradition can be a mode of analysis *and* a methodology of liberation.[18]

Similarly, Aimee Villarreal contends that ethnic studies is anthropology's "smoking mirror," "the oppositional 'native voice' that has confronted the discipline's colonial legacy and its epistemological drive to know the other."[19] Anthropologists such as Vine Deloria, Americo Paredes, and various Chicana feminists "reversed the colonial gaze," challenging anthropology's ethnographic authority, questioning the politics of authority and scrutinizing the culture concept. Yet, as Villarreal suggests, ethnic studies is often curiously overlooked even by anthropologists of migration such as Nicholas De Genova who "have called for a critical anthropology of the United States that treats the nation as a social formation built on colonialism and white supremacy."[20]

As scholar-activists, Steve and Mariela's roles as anthropologists are in constant dialogue with the critiques of marginalized voices and the knowledge that comes from the lives of colonized peoples. Mariela is a 1.5-generation immigrant (meaning children or teenagers who immigrate to the U.S. and thus often feel split between two countries), and as a Latina faculty in a U.S. applied anthropology department, she sees her role as an educator as negotiating moments of crisis or urgent situations that emerge in the lives of marginalized students and faculty. Starting in 2006 she began documenting the experiences of undocumented youth, focusing in particular on Dallas youth activists. The need to document the lives of undocumented students evolved from her own experiences as an immigrant facing deportation at the age of thirteen and the angst experienced by her family as they contemplated a forced separation.

There is no single or simple path for the researcher to take as a response to the

18. Ibid.

19. Aimee Villarreal, "Bridging the Divide Between Ethnic Studies and Anthropology," *Anthropology News* 56, no. 9 (September 2015), https://web.archive.org/web/20150926012527/http://www.anthropology-news .org/index.php/2015/09/17/bridging-the-divide-between-ethnic-studies-and-anthropology/.

20. Ibid.

challenges of the university and academy's disciplining of knowledge as part of the colonial and capitalist system, but we believe it is important to be on a path while acknowledging the contradictions we face.[21] Steve is a "white" anthropologist who has held research and teaching positions within university and non-profit research institutions. In 2010, a group of undocumented youth in Kentucky invited him to join them in D.C. to march and advocate for the DREAM Act. Since then, he has worked alongside the immigrant community in the struggle to end the detention and deportation of undocumented migrants.

Paulo Freire challenges us to consider that those of us in positions of social power are only in solidarity with the oppressed when the oppressor "stops regarding the oppressed as an abstract category … and risks an act of love."[22] Such acts can mean leaving behind some of the "securities" that a position within the colonial system provides, in order to walk alongside undocumented immigrant experts and others marginalized by the U.S. state and capitalist economic system. This is, in part, what we understand and call a methodology of *acompañamiento*. We have come to learn that this methodology of walking together becomes a way of life involving a relationship of mutuality and reciprocity towards our collective liberation. The oppressed risk an even greater act of love to walk with the oppressor. It's in these human encounters that much more than knowledge as research is discovered, but knowledge of who we are and can be as human beings. We confront the illusory and alienating realities of the myth of the American Dream that commodifies and dehumanizes all our social relations. Our struggle for liberation is fraught with ambiguity and contradictions as we live and work within the very system that we criticize and seek to transform.

21. Shannon Speed, "At the Crossroads of Human Rights and Anthropology: Toward a Critically Engaged Activist Research," *American Anthropologist* 108, no. 1 (March 2006): 66–76; Asale Angel-Ajani and Victoria Sanford, eds., *Engaged Observer: Anthropology, Advocacy, and Activism* (New Brunswick, NJ: Rutgers University Press, 2006).

22. Paulo Freire, *Pedagogy of the Oppressed* (New York: Continuum Books, 1993), 50.

Praxis-Witnessing

Engaging in unsanctioned forms of caring allows us to see and understand the practice of *acompañamiento* as an organizing strategy, a strategy of resilience and resistance, and as a pedagogical tool. Feminist scholar Leela Fernandes asks, "How do we produce knowledge about the experience and cause of oppression in ways that are non-exploitative and which do not turn people's suffering into a spectacle that we safely consume from a distance?"[23] To address these questions, she discusses representation in relation to "witnessing," which "must rest on a deep sense of ethical responsibility."[24] For Fernandes, witnessing "is a process in which the suffering of others sparks the soul of the witness."[25] This sort of engaged and intimate experience is by no means an impediment to social science. As Dorinne Kondo explains, "experience, and the specificity of my experience—a particular human being who encounters particular others at a particular historical moment and has particular stakes in the interaction—is not opposed to theory; it *enacts* and *embodies* theory."[26]

Approaching ethnography as a form of witnessing has implications beyond the ways in which ethnographers write. The practice of ethnography is fundamentally transformed when seen through the eyes of a witness. From the perspective of Steve and Mariela, writing, as an integral practice of doing ethnography, also needed to reflect the vulnerability one feels when ethnography became witnessing. And Marco, Clau, Pedro, and Fidel live a parallel vulnerability. Undocumented youth humanize their illegality through the documentation of their experiences and their stories of coming out as undocumented, unafraid, and unapologetic. There is a strong need to document "communities of memory" that bear witness to criminalization, fear, despair, and redemption.

23. Leela Fernandes, *Transforming Feminist Practice: Non-Violence, Social Justice, and the Possibilities of a Spiritualized Feminism* (Berkeley: Aunt Lute Books, 2003), 90.

24. Ibid., 91.

25. Ibid.

26. Dorinne Kondo, *Crafting Selves: Power, Gender, and Discourses of Identity in a Japanese Workplace* (Chicago: University of Chicago Press, 1990), 24.

And, in turn, these memories can play a significant role in ethnographic research. Affect has a place in ethnographic production.[27] As Chela Sandoval puts it "'love' as a hermeneutic, as a set of practices and procedures...can transit all citizen-subjects...toward a differential mode of consciousness."[28]

For these reasons, the six of us decided to author this book collectively. Rather than editing a collection of individually authored chapters, we wanted to acknowledge our solidarity while at the same time using this space to address our differences through our voices and unique experiences. We have different backgrounds, different connections, and different roles that we play in struggles for liberation. Initially, Steve and Mariela connected as anthropologists when we participated in a common session at a professional conference. We realized we were connected to many of the same friends in the undocumented-led organizing community. Pedro, Marco, and Claudia were already working, discussing, writing, and thinking about the ideas in this book in relationship with one another as friends and organizers. Fidel and Shaun were doing the same thing in the university setting with Mariela. Through continuous dialogue over time we began to envision a book that brought our stories together. However, it was the actual writing of the book itself that helped us envision a third space of possibility and to envision a tangible process to build solidarity while honoring our different voices. The Prelude and this Introduction are written mostly in the first-person plural to reflect our collective voice.

Chapter 1 is a testimonial photo essay interspersed with the words of participants in immigrant struggles. Chapters 2–5 are testimonial narratives by undocumented migrants. They are written in the first person because they are about each individual's experiences. The same is true for Mariela's story (Chapter 6). We chose the *testimonio* as a narrative style because of its long connection with struggles for liberation, its emphasis on self-authorship, and its connection to Latin America. Testimonial narratives have a

27. Virginia Domínguez, "For a Politics of Love and Rescue," *Cultural Anthropology* 15, no. 3 (2000): 361–93.

28. Chela Sandoval, *Methodology of the Oppressed* (Minneapolis: University of Minnesota Press, 2000), 139.

long tradition in both anthropology and in social movements. For example, texts like Che Guevara's *Reminiscences of the Cuban Revolutionary War* and *The Autobiography of Malcom X* are considered important first-person narratives about struggles for national liberation. In addition, *testimonio* is also linked to theories of decolonization, particularly Paolo Freire's pedagogy of liberation and third world feminisms such as *I, Rigoberta Menchú*. In Spanish, *testimonio* has both a legal and a religious meaning as it is related to the act of testifying in court or bearing witness to one's faith.[29]

These self-authored narratives are about giving witness to the lived experiences of populations who often don't have a voice or whose point of view has not been heard before by the wider public. *Testimonios* are often collected or recorded by a social scientist, journalist, or writer. It is also related to a variety of other genres: oral history, life history, autobiography, documentary novel, and the like. However *testimonio* is considered different from any of these because of the narrator's intentionality or urgency.[30] In our case, there certainly was a collective and individual urgency to share these first-hand accounts of activism, deportation, struggle, pain, and liberation. We intentionally decided to reflect the uniqueness of each voice through choice of language and organizational style. We did not follow a template.

However, we faced challenges in deciding how to string the narratives together and deciding on roles we should play in writing the book. The nature of the role of the social scientist or editor is highly contested in testimonial accounts and in ethnography.[31] *Testimonios* raise questions about the process of recording, transcribing, editing, and translating from one language to another or from oral to written text. We struggled with these questions. We wondered if and when we should write in the first or third person, in the singular (individual) or plural (collective). We struggled with editorial decisions

---

29. These insights about the *testimonio* are based on John Beverly, *Testimonio: On the Politics of Truth* (Minneapolis: University of Minnesota Press, 2004).

30. Ibid., 32.

31. Ibid., 6, 32.

about what to leave in and what to remove. We wondered about imposing our understandings on each other's narratives, and we struggled around honoring the uniqueness of each voice while still putting together a cohesive narrative.

These struggles and contradictions were also the reasons why we felt *testimonio* was appropriate. It gave the undocumented youth more control over the shape and internal logic of the book. Steve and Mariela collected the narratives presented here through discussions, observations, closed-ended and open-ended interviews, and most importantly by being involved in the events described in the narratives for over a decade. When it came time to do the actual writing, the youth felt comfortable leaving the bulk of that work to the academics, who, in any case, had privileges of time and training. Marco, Clau, Pedro, and Fidel work full time, and finding time to write was difficult. We had numerous one-on-one sessions during which we discussed the narratives as well as the goals of the book. We met as a group several times, including during a three-day writing retreat to work on the individual narratives. The process of putting together this book forced us to confront numerous contradictions and to envision possible alternatives. As John Beverly points out, "What happens in *testimonio* is not only the conversion of 'other' into an ideological signifier but also the confrontation through the text of one person (the reader and/or interlocutor) with another level of a *possible* solidarity and unity (a unity in which differences will be respected)."[32] It is, in part, by confronting and working through the struggles we faced writing this book that we experienced, collectively, one possibility for mutual liberation.

Brief Overview of the Book

The title of this book, like the rise of an undocumented-led movement for freedom, is a criticism of the mythological American Dream. It is also a break from the mainstream

---

32. Ibid., 80.

immigrant-rights organizing for the right to assimilation within an oppressive political-economic system of unequal power relations.

Chapter 1 ("Shadows then Light") is a photo essay that documents the movement of undocumented-led civil disobedience as a way of "coming out of the shadows." Its goal is to not only unapologetically affirm human dignity but also to shine light back into the shadows, where the majority of the immigrant community remains, facing the threats of dehumanization, detention, deportation, and other forms of state violence. It includes short testimonials and quotations collected by Steve (the photographer) from movement activists over the period the photos were collected.

In Chapter 2 ("The Mis-Education of the Migrant"), we share the story of Marco Saavedra's journey as he navigates education in elite schools, family life in the Bronx, immigrant rights organizing. Along the way, we learn the reasons why he chose to reject the DREAMer identity and challenge U.S. state violence through civil disobedience with acts that included infiltrating the Broward Detention Center and crossing the border with the "Dream 9." Marco's story provides a critique of mainstream liberal organizing while also holding out hope for building a movement for a new society.

Chapter 3 ("A Deported DREAMer's Story") is the anonymous testimony by a college student about being detained, deported, and trafficked back into the U.S. The story emphasizes levels and strategies of disclosure, as undocumented youth are forced to reveal their status and choose to "come out of the shadows." In addition, the story discusses the DREAMer ideal of the deserving good student that is emphasized by youth organizing in support of the DREAM Act. It compares this ideal to the realities of fear, trauma, and family separation experienced by our unnamed DREAMer.

In Chapter 4 ("Layers of Pain"), we share the stories of immigrant women in detention through the lens of Claudia Muñoz's infiltration of an immigrant detention center in Michigan. Claudia exhorts us to consider the layers of suffering within the lives of marginalized immigrant women, and she finds their roots in the structural violence caused by an unjust global economic system.

In Chapter 5 ("Brothers Crossing Borders"), we tell the stories of the Santiago brothers and their family's' disconnected connections between Oaxaca and Kentucky. Their stories speak to the precarious journey through the illusions of the American "Dream" from the perspectives of Pedro and his brother Cefe, a participant in the "Dream 9" action, who was ultimately deported. They are both Zapotec-speaking natives of Oaxaca. They leave us with the question of what freedom looks like when one is caught between the (un)freedoms of two nation states.

In Chapter 6 ("Acompañando"), we share Mariela's story of Shaun Chapa, a D-DREAMer (documented DREAMer) and ally to immigrant youth in North Texas. It includes a discussion of *acompañamiento*/accompaniment—a strategic form of counter-storytelling that renders a space of communion to challenge the loneliness and invisibility of illegality. In this and all the other chapters, we share lessons that we hope can be drawn for action, research, and other forms of collective engagement.

CHAPTER 1

Shadows then Light

"There are only two services which images can offer the afflicted. One is to find the story which expresses the truth of their affliction. The second is to find the words which can give resonance, through the crust of external circumstances, to the cry which is inaudible: 'Why am I being hurt?'"
 —Simon Weil, *Simone Weil: An Anthology*

"Where we are born into privilege, we are charged with dismantling any myth of supremacy. Where we are born into struggle, we are charged with claiming our dignity, joy and liberation."
 —adrienne maree brown

I received a gift, an invitation to learn with and struggle alongside the undocumented-and migrant-led struggle for our collective freedom. The margins where the undocumented live are more than a site of deprivation, bell hooks tells us. "It is also the site of radical possibility, a space of resistance ... a site one stays in, clings to even, because it nourishes one's capacity to resist. It offers to one the possibility of radical perspective from which to see and create, to imagine alternatives, new worlds."[1] In 2010 I first witnessed undocumented youth coming out of the shadows to publicly declare, "I am

1. bell hooks, "Choosing the Margin as a Space of Radical Openness," in *Yearnings: Race, Gender and Cultural Politics* (Boston: South End Press, 1990), 150.

undocumented and unafraid." And by March 2011, undocumented youth were declaring what has now become an iconic statement for this liberation movement, "I am undocumented, unafraid, and unapologetic." This movement into the light was not only an act of individual liberation, but also one that collectively provides a light for the oppressor to see not only their own deep alienation, but also the humanity dehumanized in the shadows of U.S. empire. The photos and words that follow are meant to accompany the stories you will read as a way of sharing this gift of light to learn to see with new eyes. The gift comes as both invitation and intervention. As bell hooks writes, "This is an intervention. I am writing you. I am speaking from a place in the margins where I am different, where I see things differently. I am talking about what I see.... This is an intervention.... Marginality as a site of resistance. Enter that space. Let us meet there. Enter that space. We greet you as liberators."[2]

I was in Seattle presenting a paper about the undocumented-led youth struggle for freedom at the annual Society for Applied Anthropology meeting in 2011 when I got a call from an undocumented youth organizer asking me if I could support a direct action in Georgia, the first of many. To join the action I would have to reschedule my flight home and leave the conference early, but this is exactly what I did. In addition to leaving an academic conference, I would soon be challenged to leave "secure" employment within the academy as well, as part of a journey of accompaniment in which I would walk alongside the undocumented and migrant community. This is not to say that all allies need to quit their jobs. But I certainly hope that the stories and images the reader encounters here will cause them to contemplate (learn to see) and consider, from a perspective of struggle at the margins, that the so-called privilege that allies use—often in good faith—is part of a larger pathology that this country must not only face, but also work to dismantle. This too is part of the eclipse of dreams and a movement from shadows to light.

This photo essay describes what we are learning in this creative space of marginality

2. Ibid., 152.

and struggle, and provides a visual glimpse of the movement we are learning to create together. It builds upon a work that Marco Saavedra and I created together in 2012.[3] The quotations that are woven among the images are from anonymous undocumented organizers describing actions and/or their own evolving ideas about activism all collected between 2010 and 2017 in an attempt to document a portion of the movement of undocumented-led civil disobedience and struggle. I hope you will see beyond the narrative of rugged heroic individual struggle by undocumented youth which is the story told by liberal mainstream media and is used in campaign rhetoric to support the American Dream mythology. But rather, in these stories from the margins, you will find examples of undocumented youth shining a light back into the shadows, where the majority of community and family members remain, facing the threat of dehumanization, detention, and deportation. And even deeper still, you will learn from these stories that this light was always already present, and in fact, was the very light that nurtured this undocumented-, youth-led organizing and activism.

The images and stories that follow reveal the dignity and joy that comes with the arduous struggle for liberation, a struggle rooted in and for a more just and loving community. The civil disobedience led by undocumented youth is just one form of struggle among many forms of everyday resistance you will read about in this book. One of the most profound acts for liberation, too often not recognized as such, is the courageous, dignified decision to cross borders to care for one's family. This is what we hope to communicate in the first image of the photo essay. The mixed-media piece is a photo of the first undocumented youth-led civil disobedience action in early 2011 that followed the failed Dream Act. On top of that photo are vinyl-cut print images of a child, a border wall, and a mother with rays of light emanating from her as the source of life/love and of another kind of disobedience to the state, one that precedes and nourishes the work that undocumented youth were creating.

3. Marco Saavedra and Stephen Pavey, *Shadows then Light* (self published, 2012), https://shadowsthen light.com/.

Over the last decade, immigrants have become one of the fastest growing populations within the U.S. prison industrial complex. The increasing criminalization of immigrants has further exacerbated the epidemic of mass incarceration through growing anti-immigrant legislation, racial profiling, and new priorities and practices for immigration enforcement. But during this same time, a movement led by undocumented immigrants is also growing and challenging mainstream advocacy efforts for comprehensive immigration reform. These immigrants want to go even further, to address root issues of racial and economic inequality. They challenge the basic and spurious justifications for the criminalization, detention, and deportation of immigrants. They challenge us to face the illusion of democracy and lies of the mythological American Dream.

With the failure of the DREAM Act to pass in 2010, there came an awakening of consciousness among some of the undocumented youth. They understood that they had been used as political pawns, held up as deserving DREAMers, the good immigrants, as opposed to their parents who were bad immigrants, even criminals. With this realization came a deeper understanding of racial economic injustice, the knowledge that the struggle for freedom and human dignity must eclipse the fight for "rights." As Simone Weil has noted, "To the dimmed understanding of our age there seems nothing odd in claiming an equal share of privilege 'for everybody'—an equal share in things whose essence is privilege. The claim is both absurd and base; absurd because privilege is, by definition, inequality; and base because it is not worth claiming."[4] She goes on to say that "thanks to this word [rights], what should have been a cry of protest from the depth of the heart has been turned into a shrill nagging of claims and counter-claims, which is both impure and impractical."[5] Through the images and stories of those who suffer, we discover the truth of our own alienation, a dehumanization we attribute to this so-called "privilege," which should more aptly be called a pathology.[6]

---

4. Weil, "Human Personality," 64.

5. Ibid.

6. Theodor Adorno said, "The need to let suffering speak is a condition of all truth." *Negative Dialectics*,

Whether the mask is labeled fascism or democracy, our great adversary remains the apparatus—the bureaucracy, the police, the military. Not the one facing us across the frontier of the battle lines, which is not so much our enemy as our brothers' enemy, but the one that calls itself our protector and makes us its slaves. No matter what the circumstances, the worst betrayal will always be to subordinate ourselves to this apparatus and to trample underfoot, in its service, all human values in ourselves and in others.[7]

As one undocumented youth explained to me, there will be no real win for immigrant justice until we connect the immigrant "rights" movement with the longhaul history of the black freedom movement. We are witnessing those connections in the intersectional solidarity work between the #BlackLivesMatter movement and the movement for #Not1More detention or deportation. Liberal efforts to solve one crisis or emergency after the next through state machinery is itself part of the bad dream we must wake up from. "The tradition of the oppressed teaches us that the 'state of emergency' in which we live is not the exception but the rule."[8] From this broader and historical perspective, one begins to see the policing and incarceration of black and brown bodies as deeply woven into the fabric of America's history of settler colonialism, genocide, slavery, Jim Crow laws and the ongoing criminalization of communities of color. There is no "just" immigration reform that doesn't, at the same time, challenge the white supremacy and anti-blackness undergirding the prison and immigration industrial complexes. There is no "immigration problem" out there waiting for well-intentioned liberals to fix it with their access to privilege. The problem is deeper still, a pathological, settler-colonial system that is still at work, not as a historical event but as an ongoing

---

translated by E. B. Ashton, (New York: Seabury Press, 1973), 17.

7. Simone Weil, "Reflections on War," *Politics* (February 1945), 55.

8. Walter Benjamin, "Theses on the Philosophy of History," in *Illuminations*, edited by Hannah Arendt, (New York: Schocken Books, 1968), 257.

historical process that requires continual violence to maintain.[9] The problem, as Marco Saavedra suggests in a poem you'll encounter later in this book, is ours: "What if the illegal is you? / Your institutions, your economy / your system of reality."

The first series of images (photos 1–9) are of undocumented-youth-led civil disobedience actions organized across the U.S. from 2011 to 2012. After the failure to pass the DREAM Act in December 2010, the National Immigrant Youth Alliance (NIYA)[10] emerged as a break-off from United We Dream, whose organizing efforts they felt had been co-opted by the Democrats, whose idea of "comprehensive immigration reform" was too narrowly focused on the "good immigrant" and further criminalized the so-called "bad immigrant" and who only backed the DREAM Act at the last minute. Further, they began to recognize that both political parties and their legislative efforts are part of the broken system that had been dehumanizing their parents and larger immigrant communities, advocating for "winnable legislation" by using the narrative of the good DREAMER/immigrant who embodied the illusion that upward mobility was available to all in the U.S. based on hard word and merit. These images document just a few of the nearly twenty direct actions across the U.S. that were part of NIYA's strategy of escalation. As they say in their mission statement: "We have reached a point where lobbying alone is not adequate to accomplish our mission. We strongly believe that our

9. Roxanne Dunbar-Ortiz, *An Indigenous Peoples' History of the United States* (New York: Beacon Press, 2015).

10. The National Immigrant Youth Alliance (NIYA), led by undocumented youth played an important role in building this movement, but we soon came to see that this was already being done by elders long before and still by others joining in creative local ways that emerged in 2013 through grassroots groups working across the U.S. in the struggle for #Not1More detention or deportation to abolish ICE. NIYA was largely active in movement organizing from 2010 to 2014. But before and after this, undocumented youth were leading work in many grassroots organizations and I can say ragtag networks in the most positive sense, of undocumented and migrant leaders doing this movement-building work, including: Georgia Latino Alliance for Human Rights (GLAHR); Juntos; Organized Community Against Deportation (OCAD); the Congress of Day Laborers; Puente in Phoenix, Arizona; Northwest Detention Center Resistance; Mijente; SOA Watch; local chapters of the National Domestic Workers Alliance; and many others.

movement needs to escalate and we will use mindful and intentional strategic acts of civil disobedience to be effective." They changed the focus of organizing from national legislative rights for themselves, to state and local struggles against injustices that the larger immigrant community was facing, including organizing against Secure Communities deportation programs, 287g laws that U.S. Immigration and Customs Enforcement used to delegate certain powers, other local and state anti-immigrant legislation, as well as the growing detentions and deportations under the Obama administration.

The next series of images (photos 13–15) are of NIYA's escalation to organizing from within detention centers and jails between 2012 and 2013. The strategy here was to risk infiltrating the institutions that most immigrants maybe feared most—prisons and detention centers—in the hope of learning from those even more marginalized in order to expose the lies of the democrats (that, while the Obama administration and most Democrats said they were advocates for Dreamers and immigrants, they were at the same time building the immigrant prison industrial complex faster than any other president in U.S. history). One of the first actions was by Marco Saavedra and Viridiana Martinez who infiltrated the Broward Detention Center in Florida where over six hundred low-priority immigrants were detained, some for up to three years. This organizing challenged the lack of implementation of Obama's own policy, outlined in the Morton Memo, to not detain or deport low-priority undocumented migrants and to grant prosecutorial discretion in all such cases.

The photo essay continues with a series of images (photos 16–21) created between 2013 and 2014 of three campaigns and direct actions that sought to return to the U.S. deported DREAMers and other low-priority undocumented family members: DREAM9 (Nogales), Bring Them Home (Laredo), and Bring Them Home (Tijuana). The photo essay concludes with a series of images (photos 22–32) of direct actions and civil disobedience led by the larger undocumented community across the U.S. to struggle against the rapidly increasing detentions and deportations under Obama between 2014 and 2016. These actions include the undocumented and immigrant-led struggles from

Pennsylvania, Washington, D.C., Georgia, Illinois, Texas, Ohio, and Arizona to call for #Not1More deportation, to shut down detention centers, to abolish ICE, to resist deportation through sanctuary, to end border imperialism, and to take their demands to both the Republican and Democratic conventions in 2016.

I want these images and stories to jar us awake so we might not only better understand the predicament we are in but, more importantly, see who we might become when love and justice shine light on what it means to become more human. The undocumented migrant community is demonstrating to us what dignity, love, struggle, and freedom look like. Another system of social relations is possible. Freedom, while a long road, is possible. The undocumented-led movement for freedom helps us along that long road by reframing the "race" and "citizenship" problem as a question of white supremacy/pathology embedded in the setter-colonial and capitalist structuring of U.S. society. We argue that the legal struggles for rights are not the only recipe for overcoming structured inequality. Rather, we should be fighting to restructure the classist and racist structures of our economy, government, and institutions to protect human dignity and freedom. And returning once again to bell hooks's invitation/intervention from the margins: she posits what we are already coming to know, through our shared collective experience, that the margins hold the possibility for a space "where we move in solidarity to erase the category colonized/colonizer."[11] Here, the colonizer who speaks about the other, or for the other—whether a politician or academic—must surrender power to engage in life and organizing with the marginalized "other." Thus, as Andrea Smith says, "a vision for immigrant rights is one that is based less on pathways to citizenship in a settler state, than on questioning the logics of the settler state itself."[12]

Illuminated then by the light of these lives, we are confronted with the complicity of our participation in a hegemonic political-economic system that begets darkness,

---

11. hooks, "Choosing the Margin," 150.
12. Andrea Smith, foreword to *Undoing Border Imperialism*, by Harsha Walia (Oakland: AK Press, 2013), xiii.

generating a shadowed oppression. The questions, now, for us, for America, we the jailers: Are we free? Are we fully human? Having seen the light, might we find our way to become human again?

* The following photo essay's captions can be found on pages 145–47.

Own, don't be owned / Unearth what all those lies disfigured; / "remember your first love" / Even if you must die a little—the renaissance beckons / A new world is kicking in the womb

Battling Silence
(abridged)

First, I was illegal
An identity given to me
By a socio-political complex
Hell-bent on forcing me to
Reject my notion of self.
Illegal is illegal, they said —
More than my age
More than my gender/sexuality
More than my humanity —
I was now this thing, an "it"
No longer a human being.
I stay silent.

* * *

Then I became unafraid,
Unashamed,
Unapologetic —
About my immigration status,
About refusing to bow down
to rhetoric & political punting,
about choosing a movement over a campaign,
about acknowledging the full, wide, deep and beautiful
spectrum of the undocumented experience,
and about reclaiming my voice and
demanding that it be the only vehicle
through which my story is told.

Kemi Bello

"And to the government, as long as there are wars and poverty there will be migrants. As long as there are people in power that benefit from deportations, there will be deportations—but there will also be those of us fighting them. And as long as there are undocumented people, there will be those of us willing to protest, willing to risk arrest, willing to risk deportation—in order to highlight the hypocrisy of the government. Because as long as there is oppression there will be resistance."

"When you bottle up your status for 20 + years and you suppress it, you're no longer telling your story, you're screaming it."

"I could be deported at any moment. Everything could be taken away from me, including the chance to be near my daughter, who is an American citizen. I have remained silent for too long. I am tired of living in fear. Silence is no longer an option."

"Every time that I compromised with the hate ... I felt that I was digging myself further into a hole."

"Getting arrested can be a terrifying experience, especially when you are intentionally putting yourself in that situation. But once you're there, looking at your biggest fear face to face, you become so completely determined and unafraid. It's a very liberating experience. It's like reclaiming your freedom in a way."

"Then all childhood arrivals said, thankfully DACA gave us life ... cause NAFTA truly fucked us. Yes, it's relief, but at what price."

In the last cell we were moved to ... we met a mother who was in deportation proceedings. Then and there is where it hit me — that could have been MY beautiful mother! At that moment I was reminded of exactly why I was in there ... We are thankful that we were released, after a night in jail, but unfortunately ... this mother will be sent back and separated from her family.

Even now, my mother is still upset that I ended up in a jail cell. That is the last place where she would have wanted to see her only daughter. She supports the movement and she understands the reasons behind it. But as she says, *Soy carne de su carne, sangre de su sangre* (Flesh of my flesh, and blood of my blood). It hurts her. She'll come around. I believe it.

Lately, I've spoken to many Dreamers that hold back from organizing because they fear the reaction of their parents. I was in this same exact situation not too long ago. Disobedient is the last word that would ever describe me. But I've come to realize that I am a part of something bigger. This movement is stronger than me and more powerful than me. It's something I cannot control. My parents are both coming to realize this as well, and we're working together to live in peace. Change has been hard on them, and change has been hard on me. But I don't regret anything that I have done thus far and I know that deep, deep down, as far as you can search into their hearts, they are proud of me as well.

Mami and Papi, if you ever read this, I want you to know that it is your love and undying courage that gives me the strength to continue to fight! I'm sorry. *No tuvieron una hija normal* (You did not give birth to a normal daughter). I Love You!!!

THOSE youth had to pay a terrible price in moral discipline, in interior effort & courage, which the country cannot imagine...

If you the American people invented the Illegal, Then you must answer Why...

& the future of the country Depends on whether or not we can face that Question

"We fear being separated from our families. We fear not seeing our parents, our brothers, our sisters. We fear not seeing them again. And so we hide. We ignore our reality, that every day is a risk. But now we are confronting that fear. As a community we can stand strong. We do civil disobedience because we are not afraid of those who persecute us."

"We don't need to assimilate into a system that oppresses us. Instead we need to challenge that system, and create a real movement, a movement where we are fighting for human rights for all."

"My very existence is an act of freedom."

"Our community is afraid to come out because of an identity created by a law. Fear is a social construct. We shall reconstruct our feelings."

"We proudly told the agents we are undocumented and we are no longer afraid of them and will no longer tolerate the hate they bring to our families. They were really confused. They couldn't understand why undocumented youth would come to ICE willingly. It felt great to confront what I was raised to fear."

"For the record, undocumented youth have been defending and standing up for our parents, and pushing the limits of what defines a "good" immigrant. It's where the term "unapologetic" comes from. We are unapologetic about our parents, the sacrifices they made, the risks they took, and the fact that we are here undocumented and unafraid."

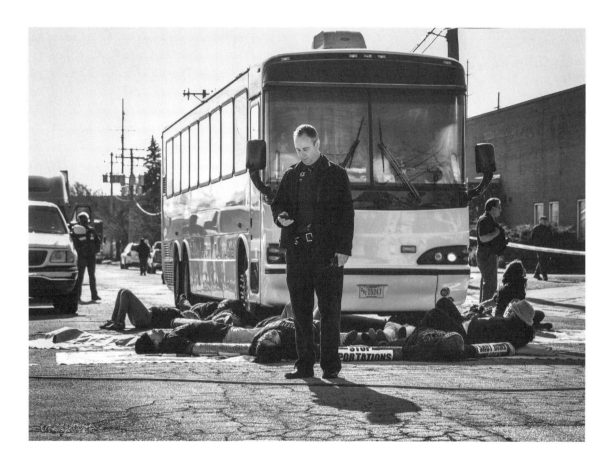

 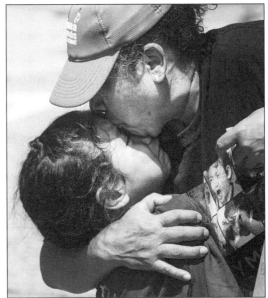

"If a society permits one portion of its citizenry to be menaced or destroyed, then, very soon, no one in that society is safe. The forces thus released in the people can never be held in check, but run their devouring course, destroying the very foundations which it was imagined they would save ... Judged by this standard, we are a loveless nation. The best that can be said is that some of us are struggling. And what we are struggling against is that death in the heart which leads not only to the shedding of blood, but which reduces human beings to corpses while they live.

"One discovers the light in darkness, that is what darkness is for; but everything in our lives depends on how we bear the light. It is necessary, while in darkness, to know that there is light somewhere, to know that in oneself, waiting to be found, there is a light. What the light reveals is danger, and what it demands is faith ... Generations do not cease to be born, and we are responsible to them because we are the only witnesses they have. The sea rises, the light fails, lovers cling to each other, and children cling to us. The moment we cease to hold each other, the moment we break faith with one another, the sea engulfs us and the light goes out."

—James Baldwin, *Nothing Personal*

CHAPTER 2

The Mis-Education of the Migrant

"When you control a man's thinking you do not have to worry about his actions. You do not have to tell him not to stand here or go yonder. He will find his 'proper place' and will stay in it. You do not need to send him to the back door. He will go without being told. In fact, if there is no back door, he will cut one for his special benefit. His education makes it necessary."

— Carter G. Woodson, *The Mis-Education of the Negro*

"The black revolution is much more than a struggle for the rights of Negroes. It is, rather, forcing America to face all its interrelated flaws: racism, poverty, militarism, and materialism. It is exposing evils that are rooted deeply in the whole structure of our society. It reveals systematic rather than superficial flaws, and it suggests that radical reconstruction of society itself is the real issue to be faced."

— Martin Luther King, Jr.

I stopped being afraid at the start of 2010, when I was twenty years old. I witnessed five youth come out, declaring they were "undocumented and unafraid," on national media in front of the Immigration and Customs Enforcement headquarters at the Federal Plaza in Chicago. The most memorable words came at the end of Reyna Wences's testimonio; crying, she said, "I'm doing this for you, for all of my people. I will not hide in the shadows any longer. I'm a human being. I deserve to be happy."[1] It was and remains quite a simple process in retrospect—a mix of imagination, hope, faith, love and most other things that make one's soul smile instead of frown. My awakening to what freedom and dignity look like happened through one friend and another and another. Seeing them coming out of the shadows, facing their fears and entrusting them to me and complete strangers, who God knows could have been unreceptive, taught me to do the same.

Trust others. Trust them with your guilt, insecurities, and shame. I confess my fears—of the terror of deportation, of finding myself irreconcilable with our present reality, of loneliness, insecurity, and depression. I've been disillusioned by promised policies of relief. I've felt liberated and then overwhelmed by organizing. Sometimes words are insufficient. But struggling for liberation is worth it. I was, and remain, undocumented—since the age of three when my sister, father, aunt, and I entered the US illegally, across the southern border, to reunite with my mother. It has taken sixteen years of schooling and countless moments of pondering to figure out that we were not to blame for this transgression. Politics, the environment, economy, hunger, and poverty all had their hands in it, as did the better future that America—the part north of Mexico—presented to my young parents.

My family had been farmers for millennia—ever since first setting foot on this continent. We had settled in what became a small village, San Miguel Ahuhuititlan, located in the rugged southern state of Oaxaca where the Sierra Madre Sur and Sierra Madre Oaxaca, the unconnected southern spine of the Rocky Mountains, unite. Most people, until recently, spoke mainly Mixteco—the native dialect. What finally made us flee north was the start of a new era; unfair and unbalanced neoliberal trade agreements between Mexico and its richer neighbors destroyed our ability to sustain ourselves. Our market—we were told—had become global, and, after a period of transition, this

---

1. Reyna Wences, Statement at an Immigrant Youth & Justice League event called "Coming Out of the Shadows" in Chicago, IL, March 10, 2010, https://soundcloud.com/iyjl-1/my-name-is-reyna.

change would eventually ensure a more vital nation and people, where wealth would trickle down to fulfill the needs of all classes. Needless to say, such wealth never came and, moreover, the hunger, debt, and suffering of the nation increased.

NAFTA and other trade agreements provided and continue to allow free flow of goods and capital across borders.[2] Unfortunately, my family's attempt to seek a livelihood that was no longer feasible in their home nation was deemed an unlawful act. I, at the age of three, became an "illegal," and today at the age of twenty-nine, I am no longer ashamed of all the past experiences that brought my family and me to this place in time. This is our home now, and we will work with our present conditions as best we can. Hoping that providence will provide, praying that the path we take will be as good as the end we seek, we have faith that, if we fail (which must happen from time to time), we can be forgiven and forgive one another. The present can present itself as a gift and the future a promise, a testament of hope.

A photograph taken of me at the age of two in Mexico arrived while I was away at Deerfield Academy, an elite Ivy League college preparatory school. Looking at it, I truly saw myself, maybe for the first time. Never had I been so tangibly confronted with who I was before I knew myself as in that moment. I wanted to reach across, breaking whatever wall, border, crucible, furnace was between me and that two-year-old, hug him, and tell him, "It will be alright, we will be alright." It was alright, but the photograph represented all I had lost, all that I needed to leave behind, all that was taken from me. It holds the promise of home. I will never let go of my inner-child's hand, and I will never let him go.

I remember when I read "Of the Coming of John" by W.E.B. Du Bois for the first time. Although written in 1903, it captured my life and continues to inform my life. It's a cautionary tale of what can happen when one is sent off by their family and community to improve oneself. It speaks of a kind of hope that is created from the dreams

---

2. Ann Kingsolver, *NAFTA Stories: Fears and Hopes in Mexico and the United States* (Boulder: Lynne Rienner Publishers, 2001).

of one's community. But it speaks of another kind of hope, of transformation, of a veil lifted, of the possibility for freedom, a hope that requires pain and struggle.

Now John was never meant to aspire to anything
He was meant to make peace with mediocrity
The others didn't think that school would spoil him
But they did wish him to become a professional
Someone who relies on statistics while working at a desk
To validate their ways
School was meant to make him understand the world:
Injustices abide—surely, but they can be justified, calibrated, charted & studied—
Mastered—
John wasn't meant to critique
To question why the world's rough ways differed so much from his folkways
John—at first—didn't judge
He accepted his own as inferior, and was ashamed whenever they would come visit
For eight long years
But after those years of assuming a position of inferiority
Some ones began hinting at his beauty through theirs
Come Out, Come Out with it:
Own, don't be owned
Unearth what all those lies disfigured;
"remember your first love"
Even if you must die a little—the renaissance beckons
A new world is kicking in the womb

Beyond the eclipse of dreams (reason)
Is the evidence of the things not seen

Beyond the church of consumption
Is a theology of freedom

The table is set.
Will you step forth & dine?[3]

The DREAM Act failed just as I was about to graduate from an elite university with credentials made for dreams. But I was developing a black consciousness, made to struggle for freedom. Paradoxically, the continuous failure of the DREAM Act did not mark the death of my dreams, but rather informed and enriched them. See the truth is, dreams never die. Dreams live and carry on, while only empires perish. Only the dreamer can abnegate the dream. No force, fear, or fraud can rip it from the sinews of my humanity. The path to freedom lies within my heart and spirit, and once you wake up and realize this, you become immortal, or mortal. You find freedom in your own sacred human dignity. I do not need to be legitimized by a particular nation-state to enact my dreams for freedom. And I, we, must practice our freedom continually, even daily. We must wake to remember and then embody the freedom that comes with awakening to our human dignity. We are not what our oppressor says we are.

Let's propose this: one wakes up, every day since the day one has consciousness, trying to justify one's existence in American society. Calculating, remembering, forcing one's legitimacy onto a reality, a story not one's own. Years pass, but your circumstances remain the same. One tires of this estrangement—can it be solely internal and individual? A decade or two permit you the opportunity and the gift to find similar others that suffer from the same alienation. Forced separation, detainment, deportation, lies, and betrayal (at times death) stand between you and life.

3. Marco Saavedra, "Of the Coming of John (After W.E.B.)," Undocumented Ohio blog, https://undocumentedohio.wordpress.com/2012/08/27/of-the-coming-of-john-after-w-e-b.

It has been said that we must be included in the American Dream in order for its promise to ring true. For as long as we have entertained this idea, we have been excluded and force-fed a nightmare—bear witness to the 256,000 deportations in 2018, to the all too common report of death along the migrant trails, and to the 42,000 immigrants on average in detention daily in U.S. prisons in fiscal year 2018.[4] Immigrants are now a fast growing segment of the expanding enterprise of the prison industrial complex. This is nothing new. If we were to truly understand the history of the American dream, we would know that it has always been at the expense of someone. And most recently, it is at our expense. Who will be next?

Of course the DREAMers had many critics. From the right, they were unlawful, invasive, parasitic refugees who feasted on the wealth of the nation. From the left, they were pawns of an irreparable system, whose lack of foresight disallowed them to see the implications of further aligning themselves with their empire. To themselves, they were true, and in that truth laid a dormant spirit, that if awakened could consume the mightiest of mountains. If this is the world we inherited, let us not be slaves. Though our poverty has granted us a plethora of dreams, let them not solely be dreams, but, rather, both by night and day let our life activity be realized within the present reality. Let us become that change we wish to see.

Failure of the DREAM Act in 2010 led to the organization of the National Immigrant Youth Alliance (NIYA), created by undocumented youth splitting off from United We Dream (UWD). NIYA members recognized that both political parties and their legislative efforts are part of the broken system that dehumanizes their parents and communities. NIYA turned its focus to grassroots organizing, using education, empowerment, and escalation, in particular civil disobedience, as strategies to build a movement rather than winning a piece of legislation. NIYA was wary of being co-opted by any political group that promised a limited piece of legislation based on the merit of the

---

4. Geneva Sands, "This year saw the most people in immigration detention since 2001," CNN, November 12, 2018, https://www.cnn.com/2018/11/12/politics/ice-detention/index.html.

"perfect" DREAMer, at the cost of continued detentions and deportations of their families. According to one of NIYA's leaders, "Maybe our goal isn't to pass the DREAM Act; maybe our goal is for undocumented youth to reach a point of acceptance, where the passing of the DREAM Act may or may not matter."[5] NIYA's mission statement read, "We have reached a point where lobbying alone is not adequate to accomplish our mission. We strongly believe that our movement needs to escalate and we will use mindful and intentional strategic acts of civil disobedience to be effective."

I am still surviving, every day, and I have decided that when you and I face our fears together, we are fearless. I decided to join in civil disobedience with NIYA in September 2011 in North Carolina to take a stand against President Obama's administration's 287(g) and Secure Communities programs, the mechanism behind growing numbers of detentions and deportations of undocumented immigrants.[6] For me and the nine other undocumented youth that were arrested, this was an act of solidarity. As I had just recently graduated from college, a privilege that less than fifteen percent of immigrant students can even consider, I realized that silence and inaction betray the immigrant community, which suffers from racist rhetoric and unjust treatment.

What NIYA realized and taught us is that there is enough power in the undocumented community to determine our future, despite whatever catastrophic history we have survived, and further, that there is enough human potential and beauty within us—something that the wider world must realize. But we first must own it.

> When they damn us to hide: we come out.
> When they tell us to follow: we lead.
> When they mire us in bureaucracy: we organize.

5. Personal field notes.
6. National Immigration Law Center, "How ICE Uses Local Criminal Justice Systems to Funnel People into the Detention and Deportation System," National Immigration Law Center website, https://www.nilc.org/issues/immigration-enforcement/localjusticeandice/.

When they tell us it is not possible: we imagine.

When we are told to stop: We fight.[7]

I remember the first night in jail. We both cried, first me, then he, and I asked him, "Why don't we go to paradise tomorrow?" He didn't answer. The question was too absurd. I thought of Mexico, maybe southern France, but really I was thinking of Christ on the cross telling the crucified criminal adjacent to him, "Today you will be in paradise." Absurd, as well, I suppose. What I mean by this is that behind the horror is the glory, one can be free while imprisoned, and that slow sullen tears sometimes turn into joy. What I discovered, maybe for the first time, hopefully not the last, is that life is ugly, yes, tragic, indeed, but beautiful too.

It may sound counterintuitive, but the most useful, dangerous, meaningful thing I did with my life was sit in a jail cell and think and panic and wonder and remember. I thought of my father's anger, of my mom who was psychologically collapsing, of my younger sister and older sister's doubt. Detention does this to families. Then the walls fell around me and I could see my father, mother, and sisters once again, anew, and I knew myself better and was happy. That alone was a challenge to those around me and above me and I was full. And this is not at all a romancing of my condition. It is my reality. The veil appeared to lift, for I knew, in those moments, my full humanity, and even yours. But time would remind me that as long as America refused to face why the illegal exists, the veil would remain.

One of the black and unknown bards of yesteryear once sang, "The very time I thought I was lost, my dungeon shook and my chains fell off"—a song that rang true while I sat in the Mecklenburg County Jail.[8] What is also true is this: one learns to die in

7. Marco Saavedra, "On Mohammad Abdollahi," Undocumented Ohio blog, https://undocumented ohio.wordpress.com/2012/04/17/on-mr-mohammad-abdollahi.

8. James Baldwin, "The Fire Next Time," in *The Price of the Ticket: Collected Nonfiction, 1948–1985* (New York: St. Martin's Press, 1985), 336.

jail, to "become all flame."[9] What I think and what I witness from undocumented youth willing to risk going to jail is that we dramatize the ordeal we have already been condemned to. This is in reality a risk we face every day. The spectacle of civil disobedience sheds the light of our humanity on the everyday lived reality of prison and oppression at the hands of the state. So we decide, it is better to go to jail than be a part of what America deems "proper" and "good." Fenton Johnson says it plainly, "I am tired of work; I am tired of building up somebody else's civilization."[10]

This relationship between us, the displaced, and entire body politic has played out many times before. The future of the illegal determines the future of the entire nation. There is no immigration problem to be solved by this body politic. The problem is the body politic. I am the problem. I am the problem that no one wants to talk about. This is our problem. Who made the illegal? Who needs the illegal? And why?

> What if upon me is a reflection of you?
> What if what you fear is who you are?
> Yes, I know myself.
> Have had to —
> otherwise I'd have to deal with
> the pathetic definitions you had for me
> and there's not enough poverty for that.
> Now, is there?
> Is there?
> Maybe the problem is ours.
> We're the problem.

9. Claude McKay, "Baptism," in *Black Voices: An Anthology of Afro-American Literature*, edited by Abraham Chapman (New York: Mentor, 1968), 372.

10. Fenton Johnson, "Tired," in James Weldon Johnson, *The Book of American Negro Poetry* (New York: Harcourt, Brace and Co., 1922), 144.

Now this sounds like a play.
With equal parts?
    What if the problem is you?
What if the illegal is you?
Your institutions, your economy
your system of reality
your gods
are now being weighed by those sullen
people you've denied so long...
    Are the scales fair?
Is fortune rigged?
Whose world will become anew?[11]

The problem (and indictment) of the undocumented illegal immigrant is a metaphor for the country. If I was never illegal, then that cornerstone on which lay the foundation for our way of life is folly. If I was never illegal, then, perhaps the economy, the international politics, multinational corporations and their unmatched revenues were never legal. If from the outset people are declared as less than human, if our own brothers and sisters are judged to be illegal, then the system of reality that justifies it is from the beginning, the source of our problems.

Politicians ignore (or misunderstand) these truths, as they turn us into talking points for comprehensive immigration reform. They completely avoided the problem we face as soon as we became DREAMers, the "good immigrant" deserving the DREAM Act. This doesn't mean the DREAM Act would not be helpful, but at what cost to our community and to this nation? We are told all thinking people support immigration reform, but should the dignity of a few "good immigrants" assimilated into the U.S. as citizens

11. Marco Saavedra, "Que?!," Undocumented Ohio blog, https://undocumentedohio.wordpress.com/category/poems/page/2.

be used to maintain empire? The proposals for so-called comprehensive immigration reform are never comprehensive and do not address the ongoing root causes of the oppression immigrants face due to empire building, from the disruptive foreign policies behind the push factors of immigration, to the criminalizing and detention of immigrants within the U.S. Political parties vie to purchase the Latinx vote, negotiating what rights to adjudicate for whom, but blind to the reality that freedom cannot be determined for other people. If you want freedom, you will have to take it, right here, right now, unconditionally. We, the undocumented, do not need legalization to be free if no human being is illegal. Our freedom is not an acquisition to be bartered for. We need not lobby or compromise with the oppressor (on the oppressor's terms and timeline) for something that could never be taken or owned by another. And the illegal indictment remains: America, the land of the free and the brave must recognize us as human beings first and foremost, but also as citizens, for it to become truly democratic, to finally be united.

The American Dream is not great. Look at what it has done to you and yours. There is nothing to its bombast but empty rhetoric and cowardly oppression. How much longer will you fawn over its empty promises, its "false gods and false means of salvation?"[12] Let me suggest this—you don't belong. Never did. The current system was designed and now operates at your expense. You were never meant to be a part of a country that promotes genocide, poverty, and pain in exchange for profit and superficial safety (which only expose the depths of its insecurity). You stand, then, as a threat, as living proof of its shamed and shammed attempt at democracy. You were less a priority than capital. You were valued better dead (preferably, never alive). You are the uncomfortable, unassimilable reminder of the great tragedy of our age, that America knows so little about what it means to be human.

You are deemed an illegal. Your humanity cannot be justified within the context of a dehumanizing body politic. You disprove the America Dream, meaning you prove that

---

12. W.E.B. Du Bois, *The Souls of Black Folk* (New York: Oxford University Press, 2007), 10.

America never was what it thought it was. And now that we know this, the growth pains must follow. We must reject the current political reality and work tirelessly and doggedly for a new, better, kinder, and equitable reality until it is formed. Come what may, we must create and recreate the world not in our or their image, but in the image of justice, love, and kindness. It makes no sense to assimilate to what is. We must keep ourselves from that monstrosity. To recreate empire is not revolutionary. I will keep myself from monstrosity.

We are human beings, and as such it is beneath us to demand what is inherently ours: the freedom to live, to work, to love, to study, to aspire, and be legitimately welcomed and accepted in our home. Yes, the outlook is grim, yes, the empire seems insurmountable, and, yes, the obstacles overabundant. But let these giants be met with our whole and true selves and our whole force of grace, faith, hope, and forgiveness. Come what may, it is our uninterrupted duty to reclaim not only our own, but our enemies' humanity so that posterity inherits not a more genteel, but a gentler world.

If a system is broken, then it can't be reformed, but must be reinvented entirely. This is something the myopic American mentality cannot imagine (much less understand) because it means the dismantling of the current power dynamic, the end of the American empire and nightmare, inherited from Europe. The way we start is by applying counter-intuitive means to counter-hegemonic ends. It means we have no party loyalty, as our faith is not guaranteed by any of the current institutions. If they haven't yet healed the catalog of injustices in the past, there is no reason to believe they will do so now. Our end goal should not be for the right to integration. We have been integrated for a very long time, unjustly. Integration is the problem. Do I need legalization or does America need to stop justifying systemic catastrophe?

It is only recently that we've heard a new discourse surrounding migrants, one about human dignity. This has not been brought about by any change in legislation, executive action, charity, or nonprofit timeline, but, instead, by a new beat being sounded by our disenfranchised community itself. We are undocumented, unafraid, and unapologetic! We are resisting anti-immigrant legislation, and challenging rhetoric, policies, and practices that criminalize us. We are demanding "not one more deportation" and an end to the immigrant detention complex. DACA was not a sign of good things to come, but rather, a token response to our demands after we occupied and closed down President Obama's re-election campaign offices in Colorado, Michigan, Ohio, California, and nearly so in Georgia and North Carolina. We can learn from those before us, those enslaved by U.S. empire, who sang, "If I had-a- my way, I'd tear this building down."[13] We, the undocumented and unafraid, are half-dead, but that means we are still alive. And what we have left to live is a witness, a testimony of our times and our future, which appears cold and lonely, but also beautiful and gay.

"Do you know what makes the prison disappear?" asked an artist and prophet of long ago. I believe with van Gogh that the prison begins to disappear with every deep, genuine affection; it disappears when we are friends, brothers, and sisters, and when we love.[14] Love removes the illusions and masks we are forced into. Love allows one to see in full, know in full, without our present-day distortions. Love reconciles our deep alienation from ourselves, and from one another. Love knows that no one is innocent, but all are redeemable. Love knows persons are complete, prone to divinity, prone to failure and in that crucible we are formed.

Perhaps we have focused too much on the end goal and lost sight of how we progress and the process itself. Maybe the process itself can be our end, being and becoming a beloved community.

If you cannot justify our present reality, then you will become illegal, too. You will be irreconcilable with the present. That's the education I gained organizing inside and

13. Anonymous slave song quoted in James Baldwin, *No Name in the Street* (New York: The Dial Press, 1972), epigraph.

14. Vincent van Gogh, "July 1880, Letter to Theo," in *Van Gogh's Letters*, edited by H. Anna Suh (New York: Black Dog & Leventhal Publishers), 17. Original quote: "Do you know what makes the prison disappear? Every deep, genuine affection. Being friends, being brothers, loving, that is what opens the prison, with supreme power, by some magic force."

outside both prisons and borders (which are nearly the same): that the current system, this body politic, is unsustainable and yearns for a new creation. There is hope if you learn my name and recognize my humanity. We forget that you and me are inextricably linked, that one depends on the other. We lose when we devalue ourselves and dehumanize others because we have been taught to hate so much. We must be careful not to discard analysis for activism, to lose sight of ourselves in the intensity of the work. The trauma we have witnessed and experienced has taken a deep toll on us. It is too hard, too hard, too hard. Once you realize or, even worse, are forced to realize that America has tried to sequester, depress, stymie, lie, detain, and deport you and yours and that you've survived and hopefully overcome—you realize that she will continue to do so, in even more creative ways to others, and to others yet unborn. That is when the sadness begins. And that is why joy—real substantive joy—becomes even more desperately necessary, not as an escape but as an answer.

CHAPTER 3

A Deported DREAMer's Story

"They are willing to endure misery and dangers for months on end. They come armed with their faith, a resolve not to return...and a deep desire to be at their mothers' side."
—Sonia Nazario, *Enrique's Journey*

I remember the day my mother left my father. The violent scene that occurred just before we left our home still plays vividly in my mind. I know that it happened, it wasn't a dream. It's true because my mother corroborated the event to me on numerous occasions.

The gate was open as my mother literally fought for her life against my father. The only witnesses were my eldest brother and me, the youngest of seven siblings. I remember myself trying, without success, to pull my father back. He had my mother by the hair and held her against her will. When she was able to break loose, my father grabbed a rock that would kill anyone instantly. As he held the rock, ready to smash it against my mother's head, my older brother pulled the rock from behind him, making him fall along with it. I don't know where the rest of my brothers were while the altercation was happening—at school probably.

I remember leaving our home and riding the 1960s-era buses still in use today in rural parts of Guerrero, Mexico. We left my birthplace, and moved to my aunt's home about an hour away. I do not recall my birthplace prior to my deportation; it was only when I was deported that I was able to "visit" my birthplace. I needed birth certificates to bring back to the U.S. for when the need arose. I was struck, as the taxi driver drove through some street, by an adobe building. The black and white letters read Museo de Antropología (Anthropology Museum). I did not venture inside; one of the things I regret, but at the time the goal was to come back home to the U.S. I had started my first semester as an anthropology student at University of North Texas, and I never thought that a few weeks into it I would be deported.

Driving by the museum made me so happy. At a time of distress and anguish, not sure if I would be able to go back home to the U.S., I took it as a sign from the heavens above that I would return. I understand that this may not make sense to some, but in dire circumstances, I have learned, we start to believe in things we don't normally believe. The town where I was born is quiet; there was hardly anyone in the plaza where people usually gather. In many of the stories my mom still tells us, there is a tree. I saw the tree that had seen my mother when she was still living with my father. There are black benches scattered around the plaza, and bougainvilleas with flowers of different hues adorn parts of the street. The church is painted in white complemented with soft colors. I was there for an hour or two, but it felt as though I lived there all this time thanks to my mom's stories.

The plaza is neatly kept. The majority of the streets are paved, but some remain dirt roads. Mango trees are everywhere. I can only imagine how beautiful they must look when they have plenty of fruit hanging from their branches. My birthplace is located twenty minutes from the major city of Iguala, infamous now for the disappearance of forty-three students who've yet to be found, and a thirty-minute taxi ride from my aunt's home.[1] When I think about my birthplace I feel the need to know more about it, to walk its streets, but I can't because I am undocumented. However, my mom usually talks

---

1. On September 26, 2014, forty-three students from the Ayotzinapa Rural Teacher's College disappeared. Their disappearance sparked national demonstrations and international outrage over alleged government complicity. The film *Ayotzinapa: Chronicle of a State Crime*, directed by Xavier Robles, explores the involvement of police, state authorities, and Mexican elites.

about it when I ask questions. I can't help but be overcome with sadness too, because it is in this town that I hardly know, that my family's separation began. I also remember the cattle, which is odd because I was so little at the time. But I remember some cows that I know had to be my favorite. My mother and father along with all my siblings lived in a stable that had a small house where they took care of the cattle and other farm animals that belong to my godfather.

I don't have an emotional attachment to the city where my aunt and now my mother each own a house, as I do to the small town perched in the mountains of Guerrero and my birthplace. I lived in the city where mom has a home now for a few months and I only visited once or twice a year for no more than three days, also, it was there where I spent the last months before migrating to the states. Although I lived in the town where I was born only until I was two and a half years of age, my father's family still lives there, and it is the place that my mother talks about the most.

I remember asking my mother to show me the bleeding wounds my father inflicted in her head. She didn't refuse each time I asked her, which were a few too many times. The last wound was bloody, my mother's hair uncombed as if she had woken up in a hurry and couldn't take care of her hair that day. There was dried blood along her hair and it still looked fresh, it was a deep wound and it was easily visible. It was on her right side, right above her ear.

Someone told me that the most violent events in our lives are the ones we remember the most. I was nearing three years of age at the time of their separation, and this is all I can recall from that period of my life. All this happened between 1984 and 1985.

After my father and my mother separated she looked everywhere for work, but it was impossible to find something that would allow her to earn sufficient money to take care of seven children. It is difficult to find a decent job in Guerrero; most women end up washing clothes for a few pesos, and my mother knew that would not be enough to support us all. She moved temporarily to Mexico City, and she worked there for a few months as a maid. Then, one day she showed up to say goodbye, she was going to *el norte*/the U.S. She was leaving and we didn't know how long it would be before we would see her again. My grandparents took us in. My brothers missed our mother greatly, it took them a few months to get used to the fact that she left and that it would be a while until she came back. Our grandmother tells us that we used to cry at night and she tried to comfort us however she could, sometimes to no avail. It was a massive change for all of them. I do not know what my mother went through emotionally, but for my grandparents it was very difficult.

I have faint memories myself of this period of our lives. Seeing grandmother as my mother figure made it easier for me not to miss my mother. I wasn't missing my mother as much, I suppose, at least not as much as my brothers were. I have a sister who took care of me after my mother left. She must have been twelve years of age.

The town where my grandparents took us in is where we lived until I was twelve years old. I was also the last one to remain at my grandparents' house. This small community is located in the mountainous region of Guerrero, a small town. This is where I grew up. This is the place my grandmother and grandfather have called home for all their lives. An idyllic place situated in a valley surrounded by mountains covered with high eucalyptus trees, and pine trees among other flora that perfume it with a scent that can only be experienced there. The mornings are cold and misty, the sun showers the town with its rays and it reveals all sorts of colors. The river that provides the irrigation water for the people who plant corn and other crops flows right though the town. It also serves as a form of entertainment for local children who play in its pools. I played there too.

The small town has no more than a thousand inhabitants, everyone knows each other, and many are family members. They were born there, and still call it home today. Routine is the norm; there are no jobs but the ones people create themselves. Most of the people are farmers; corn is the most harvested crop in the town. Some fruits and other things are grown there as well, but tortillas are an essential part of the meals hence corn is planted each rainy season. Each season everyone hopes that the harvest will provide enough to last until the next rainy season. I remember times when the harvest died from either drought or floods, killing the farmers' crops, making their lives even more difficult.

I went to school in this small town in Guerrero from kindergarten to primary school. It was fun. I remember that we would go on excursions to learn about the different flora native to our state. They were basically picnics just to get out of the classroom, an excuse for teachers to get out of school too. Nonetheless, I think that was a great learning experience. In primary school, dance was part of extracurricular activities. First, one teacher would gather volunteers to make up the dance group. We would then learn how to dance *Danzas típicas* or folk dances from Mexico. My favorite was "Los Viejitos" (The Old Men). I loved the costumes, they're spectacularly colorful, and the dance can be pretty funny.

Some people in the town own small businesses that help them earn enough to survive. My grandfather was the only carpenter in town and the only one around the area. His craftsmanship was sought by people who wanted durable furniture. Of course, the furniture he makes is not your typical furniture. My grandfather knows people in town earn little money and either the dining table or the chairs or armoires he makes for them need to last for a long time if not a lifetime. What he does is "guaranteed" to last for years—if well cared for, of course.

My grandfather makes all kinds of furniture, but what I recall most are the chairs, probably because making them required collaboration between my grandfather and grandmother. I helped but I can't take credit for their work, I only helped my grandfather polish the wood before assembling it. The rest of the work was too intricate; I never learned it. Some of the chairs, that were also pricier, were painted in bright colors. My grandmother made *petates* (straw mats) that needed straw of different colors. She would twist the straw as if she was rolling a cigar, then she weaved the straw to make designs. The end result is a work of art. I remember that many of my grandpa's customers always complimented my grandma for her work. In fact, when someone needed decorative chairs, they came to him and requested that my grandmother weave them.

People live very humbly and make ends meet one way or another. The unity I witnessed first-hand in this town is something I know I will not witness again, certainly not in a big city such as Dallas. For example, when a person of lesser means dies and there is no way the family member can pay for the funeral, the town comes together and makes sure that the person is buried properly. My grandfather always makes the coffins for those who cannot afford one. And it isn't only during difficult times that the town comes together, but also during times of celebration like the patron saint's celebration, a wedding, or, as was the custom at my grandparents' home, to welcome visitors with food and send them off with food. I didn't know how fortunate we were to live with my grandparents, not until now as I write these lines. When people came to visit, I remember my grandmother always gave them something. She gave away eggs, maize, beans; anything we had she'd give. There was always something for her to give out as a gift for the visitors.

My mother went back a couple of years after she left for the U.S. She was one of many who benefited from the amnesty President Reagan passed. The Immigration Reform and Control Act (1986) legalized certain undocumented immigrants who came to the U.S. undocumented and did not have a criminal record. My brothers were ecstatic about her arrival each time. However, her visits were never more than two weeks and the sadness in their faces was palpable a day before her departure. I know they cried many nights after she left. I didn't recognize my mother when I saw her, and I was used to calling my grandmother mom instead. Someone had to explain why grandmother was grandmother and mother was mother.

As time passed and we were grown-up, each of my elder brothers started leaving my grandparents' home and moved into my aunt's house. Most of them went to school there and others went there to work. Eventually my mother was able to gather the means needed to bring us to the U.S. with her. My brothers moved to the States starting in 1993. They gained their residency or, as it's commonly called, Green Card in 1996. I remember that very well because that was the year my brother and I arrived to the U.S. My mother first brought my oldest brother to the U.S. and he was the first to obtain his Green Card. Three more followed and, three years later, she brought my brother and I, the two youngest of seven children. My sister married at a very young age and she joined us years later but returned home a few years after.

 Before I came to the States, I lived for a short period of time with a friend of my mother who took care of me and one of my brothers who is a couple of years older than me. I was about twelve and he was fourteen. We lived with them for a few months before we came to the States. My aunt who lived there moved to the U.S. for a while and decided to go back; she lives in Mexico now. My grandparents still live in the small town in the mountains of Guerrero, a place they refuse to leave. They are now in their early nineties and live by themselves. They refuse to leave their hometown, because they wouldn't have all the things they're used to, like raising chickens for example.

 My mother arrived to pick us up one day. It seemed rushed and I learned later that was because she had to go back to work quickly and my brothers were staying alone in Dallas. I was excited to come live with her, but I was sad that I was leaving my grandmother behind. She had been a mother to me all these years and now I was leaving her. As a grown man now I can only imagine how tough it must have been for her. It was very tough for me.

 I remember my grandmother came to say goodbye to us in the city where my aunt lives. The day she was going back I was the one who had to take her to the bus stop. We both were very sad. As we finally said goodbye, I remember her telling me to be on my best behavior and to not do anything bad, by this I knew she meant for me not to start drinking or doing drugs. She always emphasized the idea of studying. I remember she told me to study. She is the woman to whom I give credit today for my wanting to attend college. I remember her saying that if I wanted to be a *burro* not to study. She dried the tears from her eyes, as did I. I waited for the bus to be out of sight; the woman who I called mother was leaving and I didn't know that it would be thirteen years until I saw her again. Just as I remember the day my mother left my father, I remember the day I said goodbye to my grandmother.

My mother had already arranged all the details to bring my brother and me with her. Unfortunately, we were brought as many came to the U.S., undocumented. The two-day and one-night trip from the state of Guerrero to the state of Tamaulipas was long and extremely tiring. Northern Tamaulipas shares a border with Texas. We arrived there in mid-April. It was a clear and very hot day, but I was used to it because we used to live in a very dry and hot place. The date, to be more exact, was April 16, 1996. We were welcomed to my mother's friend's brothers' house and we were hungry but we were told there was no time to eat and that we would eat on the American side of the border. The smuggler picked up my brother no more than an hour after we arrived in Tamaulipas, to help him cross the Rio Grande. My brother and I were separated there; I remained with my mother the whole the time.

We stayed at one of the smuggler's houses waiting to hear about my brother. All the cellphone conversations about his whereabouts confused me. It was a very intense situation and I could tell my mother was extremely worried, but at that point there was nothing that she could do. We were waiting for news that my brother was already on the U.S. side so that he could be picked up by the smuggler who smuggled me and take us both to Dallas. The wait seemed to go on forever. All this started around noon. It wasn't till around 6pm that we finally got a phone call that my brother had made it across the river and he was on U.S. soil. I thought he was lucky, but my brother was less fortunate than I was: he had to swim the Rio and walk for a while.

Before we received the phone call that said my brother made it to the U.S. I was asked to learn name, date of birth, and other commonly asked questions by U.S. Customs. I learned all the answers, and I was given instructions on how to behave if there was a lot of questioning. I was ready after an hour or two of rigorous studying and quizzing. Finally we were ready to go, it was past 6pm. The sun was going down and while we drove it got dark. I remember there were five of us: the smuggler, her two kids, my mother, and I. When we got to customs the smuggler got out some documents—I didn't know at the time that they were birth certificates—and showed them to the officer. My mother got her Green Card out and handed it to the officer as well. He didn't ask any of us any questions, and the only thing I remember him asking was if we were Americans and she answered yes. The officer gave back all the documents and allowed us to go on. We had made it to the first checkpoint, but we had one more to go. I still had not seen my brother yet. I must have been asleep for the second checkpoint because when I woke up my brother was already in the car with us. We were told that we were stopping somewhere for food. It was the first time I had fried chicken, which my palate hated (I think it was right there I went back to my home in Guerrero where I always ate fresh food and home-made tortillas). We had finally made it to the U.S.

When we arrived we lived in a trailer park where my brothers and mom lived. It was a very crowded house, but that was our home and, as far as I can remember, it was comfortable. I remember this time as one of the most memorable times in my life. My brothers and I shared a room, a tiny room, in which we stayed. We would stay awake very late at night almost every night until they moved out, reminiscing about our days together when we lived with our grandparents. Many times we remember the things that we enjoyed and definitely the ones we did not enjoy, like waking up at 6am on a daily basis for example. My grandfather believed in waking up before the rooster crows. My mother held three jobs at one point while we were growing up. We hardly ever saw her except when she arrived home late, way past our bedtime. Seldom did she scold us for being too loud at night, even on the days that she had to wake up early in the morning to go to work. However no matter how late we stayed awake we had to get up early and go to school. My mother was not a happy woman when she was called to school to discuss our behavior, if bad. At this point we understood that she couldn't miss a day of work because that only made things harder for her. I think subconsciously we realized that, and we never needed her to be after us to get ready to go to school. Also I don't recall her being called to have a meeting with the principal of our school or our teachers. In part I am most positive that it was thanks to our grandparents instilling in us a sense of responsibility for ourselves.

When my brother and I arrived on April 17, 1996 to our new home, the school year had already begun and we had to wait to be enrolled. So we had some free time to do absolutely nothing. Possibly trying to adjust to our new surroundings, we made friends with kids in the neighborhood; of course, one of the things that was most noticeable was the language barrier. We didn't speak English at all and everyone we encountered spoke it. It was frustrating to need a translator for everything. As children we get annoyed by things that aren't fun, translating is one of them.

Our lives progressed in seeming normalcy. While we could never forget our undocumented status, we could sometimes ignore it. Then, in 2008, while driving back home from college, I was pulled over and subsequently detained and taken into custody by local authorities. The reason for my detention was the inability to provide a driver's license. I was held in the city where I lived then and still do now. Minor traffic violations or even simple encounters with the police can have dire consequences for people like me. This has increased the fear in local communities, where simply taking care of daily activities can put you in dangerous situations. The criminalization of daily living, *lo cotidiano*, is not unique to undocumented immigrants. Indeed, black communities, particularly black men, experience this persecution and live daily life with the fear of incarceration and even death. The places we call home are no longer safe and no longer ours.

I was transferred to the county jail a few miles north. The state of Texas requires a Social Security number to issue a valid driver's license. Because I do not have a valid Social Security Card ICE put a hold on me. This meant that I would be released to ICE.

Eventually, when I was released from jail, I was taken by ICE to their office in Dallas where ICE enters into the system all those individuals, like me, who are here in the country undocumented. The feelings I felt in there were frightening, at least they were to me. In a room where I was kept, which can be compared to one room of a two-bedroom apartment, held at least twenty-five individuals, who also had to share one bathroom while the rest of the detainees went on with their conversations.

There I heard conversations I had not heard before. Perhaps the moment in which we are marked, our personhood stamped as an entity, is transformative because it is a moment when life as we know it ends or, if we are lucky, is put on pause. We realize that we are no longer who we thought we were and that the reality we envisioned for ourselves was just a dream. We hope for something bigger, we think of what it was, and we see ourselves with no future.

Each person was called by their name, entered into the system, and given the chance to make one phone call. I called my brother. Once your name has been called and you were in the system you were ready to be sent back. I felt horrible making that phone call because it was in that moment that I knew there was absolutely no possibility that I could remain in the country. I had just signed my voluntary departure. For a system that sees a criminal, it is their version of admission of guilt. For someone who has lost their humanity, it is the point at which the image of the self as it once was collides with the image of the criminal.

I was in tears, and I couldn't even speak a sentence, soon I had to hang up because my "time" was up. The process of deportation is incredibly painful in every sense of the word. Although I feel I didn't commit a crime, I was treated as though I was a dangerous criminal; I was literally chained from head to toe. I didn't know what waited for me in Mexico, but I knew I was on my way to find out. By now it had been years since I lived in Mexico, so it all seemed strange to me. Though I have my grandparents, my sister, and other siblings, my closest family all reside in the United States. And, despite the U.S. effort to send me "home," I knew I was leaving home. The plane arrived mid-afternoon in El Paso, where all the deportees were to be released across the border into Ciudad Juárez in Mexico. I didn't know what to do; I mean, what do you do in a city that has been plagued by so much violence that, the minute you get there, the first thing you hear is advice not to get into just any taxi because you might be kidnapped?

I was afraid, genuinely afraid. Lucky for me there was a group of men who were also headed towards the southern states in Mexico. I was bound for Querétaro, where my sister waited for me to arrive. When we went to purchase the bus tickets in Juárez, we were then told to get in a car that the lady who sold us the tickets trusted. He took us to the bus stop, or close to it: he stopped across from the bus terminal and told us to cross fast and to not let ourselves be seen. I didn't know who was supposed to see us, but I am glad no one did.

Once I saw myself in Mexico, and remembered the life I had left behind I started to panic. I may have suffered depression but no one really cares about depression in Mexico. I missed school the most, and of course my family here in the states. I enjoyed seeing my sister, and my grandparents whom I hadn't seen in over thirteen years, but the sad look on my face couldn't be erased. For the first few weeks I was coping with my new home. Later, I started to miss the place I had called home most recently. I was finding myself crying for no apparent reason then. Now I know there were a lot of reasons, one was I couldn't find a solution to my dilemma, finishing my higher education in the States seemed unattainable now, and going back was something I knew would take a while.

I was home and yet home seemed like a strange place I barely knew. I wanted to go back to the United States as soon as possible, but that had to wait, as arrangements were still in the works for me to come back home.

The experience, while in Mexico, was more bitter than sweet. As happy as I was to finally see my sister, nieces and nephews, and above all my grandparents, I was sad as well. I couldn't hide my sadness. I couldn't lie to my grandmother. She was surprised that I didn't have proper documentation to live legally in the United States; she knew most of my family members had legal status.

I stayed with my grandparents for about two weeks but I had to leave when I could not hide my emotions anymore and my grandmother worried too much about my well-being. She mentioned to me that I looked sad, asking if I wasn't happy there. Of course I was happy to see them, but those were not the circumstances I had envisioned when I imagined seeing them again. I felt like I failed in every way possible. I arrived empty handed with nothing but the clothes I had on when I was arrested. It was difficult leaving the small town where I grew up, and my grandparents most of all. However, it wasn't healthy for my grandmother or me to stay with them any longer. I left not knowing when, if ever, I'd see them again. That's very difficult to live with.

I went back to the state of Querétaro for only a few weeks. My mother and I reunited in Guerrero after she had gathered all the money needed for me to come back. I didn't have any other options but to wait and be patient. The days I spent in Querétaro, I vaguely remember them. I was ill for some time, and when I wasn't ill, I was depressed. But depression fully set in when my mother arrived in Mexico, and there was no due date for me to come back. I had to come up with the money myself in order to come back to the U.S. I was finding myself crying out of nothing. Desperation, anguish was all part of me during that time. I would visit my niece who lives in Guerrero, she would comfort me when she saw I was sad, but there were days that it was too unbearable.

I mentioned to one of my friends that I was having a hard time adjusting. She advised me that, whenever I felt the need to cry, to just head over to a church and pray. Church became my hiding place from that day on. I found the light that was taken away, and I began to loosen the hold that had been put on my life. It is no wonder that churches have become part of a *santuario* movement, where undocumented immigrants find the light that has been obscured by a system that refuses to see us for who we are.

When I had finally gathered the money through friends and family members, the day I was to come back home seemed more plausible. It was the last week of July that we started the trip back, my mother and I headed north to the U.S. I met the *coyote* as soon as we arrived and I was able to install myself in the hotel. Things moved fast, and I would quickly find myself swimming the river that, before, I had only seen on the news. The same river that my brother crossed when I first came to the U.S. as a child. We tried many times and we failed just as many. A friend of mine mentioned to my mother that someone else could help me cross the border. He seemed more reliable. When changing *coyotes*, one has to be careful, for taking someone else's business can have deadly consequences.

So we left the hotel in a mysterious way; we had to tell the receptionist that we were headed next door for lunch. That didn't seem unusual because we had done that before. It was then that we met the other smuggler. The day that we swapped smugglers we were taken to his house. We waited there for a day or two until, as he kept saying, "*se calmaran las cosas.*" I think we were being sought by our previous smugglers. I do not know this for a fact, but I did get many hints that that was indeed the case.

When things "calmed down," I was sent to meet the person who would only help us across the river. We tried all day to cross the Rio Grande; it was a hot and sunny day in July of 2009. When night was setting in, we tried our very last time and we made it across. I was happy, but I knew we still had other things that waited for us, one checkpoint, for example. Someone in a truck picked us up. We were then taken to a nearby hotel where all the individuals that had made it across were to be distributed to different people to be taken to their final destination. I waited for arrangements to be made for my transfer to San Antonio, by the wife of one of the smugglers. We rode a van that transports people from Laredo to San Antonio. I had absolutely no identification and nothing but the clothes I had on that the host let me borrow. They were way too big, if I had to stand up for questioning the pants would have fallen down.

We went through the checkpoint, the immigration agent pulled the van aside and proceeded to inspect underneath the van. After that, we were asked to take our identifications out; I had nothing so I had nothing in my hand to prove who I was. I was relieved when the agent didn't see me not holding anything in my hand, and he said we were clear to go.

I arrived in San Antonio. The person who went by the nickname of EL Diablo picked me up from the bus stop where I was left by the wife of the smuggler in San Antonio. He drove me to Austin. A family member was to hand him the last amount of money owed to him in order to release me to my relatives who drove from Dallas to Austin. My relatives met me and El Diablo at a gas station where they paid the smugglers, after that I was able to come home to Dallas. When he had the cash he went back to his Hummer and politely said if I ever needed to cross again just to call them. My relatives and I headed home to Dallas after the deal was completed. It was August 4th when I made it home again.

CHAPTER 4

Layers of Pain

"Ships at a distance have every man's wish on board. For some they come in with the tide. For others they sail forever on the same horizon, never out of sight, never landing until the Watcher turns his eyes away in resignation, his dreams mocked to death by Time. That is the life of men. Now, women forget all those things they don't want to remember, and remember everything they don't want to forget. The dream is the truth. Then they act and do things accordingly."
—Zora Neale Hurston

Suffering and Pain—The Women and Me

I cannot look at photos of my mother on social media because I break down. My chest literally feels heavy and tears start flowing down my face no matter how much I try to stop them. And every time I find myself saying, "you have to be strong, this is the price you pay. You were born in a fragmented way, therefore, your heart will be forever split." But this doesn't help. I see my mom's face, now in her mid-70s, a face that I mainly see through photos because, when I left her side, she was in her late 50s. My mother, so beautiful, the light of my life, now looks much older. I can see things on her face I hadn't seen before I left, and I ask questions I never asked before. How many layers of pain does she have in her soul, I wonder? My mother who could only attend school up until the first grade, whose father abandoned her when she got very ill as a baby, who grew up so financially poor that she didn't wear shoes until she was six or seven years old, whose mother went to the city and married an abusive man who could at least afford shoes for her younger children, who learned how to read and write in her 40s when I started going to school, who raised nine children on the salary of a man who, for many years, drank almost as much as he worked. My mother—how many layers tell your story? How many layers will tell mine?

I have to say that up until I sat in a cold jail cell in Michigan, almost in complete darkness, that I had spent little time pondering these so-called layers of pain or stages of trauma. I knew before then that people go through many issues and problems throughout life, but it was hard for me to think of these many issues as trauma on top of trauma because it seems that, often, there is one traumatic event that overpowers all others. As a community we have done a poor job at seeing people, especially women, as multidimensional. I mostly embraced the idea of trauma being linear or one dimensional because, when I joined the immigrant rights movement in 2001, there was a notion within immigrant groups that the biggest problem undocumented people had was in fact, being undocumented. For instance, in various groups, when we shared our stories, nearly all of them focused on the trauma that being illegal had on our lives.[1] So it was encouraged and almost suggested that our narratives focus on that. There were times when people mentioned poverty or violence in sharing groups, but in the early days of the DREAMer movement, around 2001–2002, poverty and violence were talked about as something you left in your home country and not something that one had to talk about in America. This, of course, is a lie because abuse and violence against

1. Claudia chooses to call herself an illegal immigrant. Though she understands that it is wrong to attempt to make the existence of a person illegal, it is not her problem to rid America of the oppression it creates to feed itself. Therefore, Claudia chooses to live like the nuance she is to this country. She believes that using "illegal" instead of "undocumented" reflects more accurately on her experience living in the United States and the complexity that it is to live with a heavy label that attempts to make all aspects of her life illegal. She uses "undocumented" when people choose to use that word for themselves, and though she is undocumented herself, her resistance is not exclusively tied to documents, therefore, the term "illegal" is used throughout this chapter to fully reflect her daily experience in the U.S.

marginalized women of color in American history is as old as America itself. I later realized that this perpetual silence regarding abuse and violence against women of color existed because in many ways, the population most targeted by abuse and violence in America is black and indigenous women. And as I evolved and disengaged from the larger immigrant rights movement, I realized further that the movement was largely equating the American Dream with whiteness. For many of the organizations and people involved, any suffering and pain of immigrant women of color that was not directly related to their immigration status was inconvenient.

Infiltrating the Layers

> "I know what the world has done to my [sister] and how narrowly [s]he has survived it. And I know, which is much worse, and this is the crime of which I accuse my country and my countrymen, and for which neither I nor time nor history will ever forgive them, that they have destroyed and are destroying hundreds of thousands of lives and do not know it and do not want to know it."
>   — James Baldwin

I turned myself into immigration authorities in Detroit, Michigan, in order to be sent to a detention center.[2] In 2012, President Obama, under enormous community pressure, announced a set of deportation priorities. According to the president of "hope," only people who had committed serious crimes were going to be deported in order to better allocate financial resources and prevent the deportation of people deemed as "low-priority" who had strong links to the United States. Many people, like myself, did not think that anyone at all should be a priority because, once we accepted that one group

---

2. Aura Bogado, "Undocumented Youth Infiltrates Another Immigrant Detention Center," *The Nation* (April 15, 2013), http://www.thenation.com/article/undocumented-youth-infiltrates-another-immigrant-detention-center/.

of immigrants was more deserving of staying than another, we were opening up the door for the administration to decide who was worth keeping and who was not. Even though we didn't agree with prioritizing any group for deportation, we knew that the so-called priorities were only put out for PR purposes, so we decided to focus on that and make it very public. As different groups of undocumented youth in the country were organizing against the massive amounts of deportations that the Obama administration carried out, we saw again and again that people who, according to Obama, were low-priority, were still being deported. In 2012, undocumented immigrant youth decided to test Obama's priorities by going into detention centers undercover. Of course, because only undocumented folks could be detained, this also meant that deportation was a real possibility for us. Still, we believed that our place was anyplace the community was, including detention centers. When it became clear that President Obama had made it one of his administration's top priorities to deport as many people as possible, we knew that, as people who had a ninety percent higher chance of being detained and released than most people who were detained given our strong community ties, knowledge of organizing, the English language, and the system, it was our absolute moral duty to expose the administration from the inside.

My first night in jail was very dark and cold, an indication of the days to come. I turned myself in at the Canada Bridge in Michigan and it took nearly five hours for the ICE officers to process me. It was almost as though they had found a treasure and they had to thoroughly examine it before they claimed victory and possession of it. Once they took me to a small room in the back of the building, I realized that there was something similar about all the ICE officers I encountered that day. They were all self-righteous and felt that, in finding me, a Spanish-speaking illegal woman from Mexico, and detaining me, they had done something heroic, a great service to their great country. If I was to be successful in my task, I had to relate to them in that manner. That's when the humiliation began, a humiliation that for some reason seemed familiar to me. The cruel and humiliating words I heard from the arresting officers were new but the feeling was old.

When the female officer put on gloves and touched every part of my body uninvited, I was frightened. I didn't want her to touch me at all. I wanted to scream, to run, to break free, but the dynamics had been established, and her firearm was visible. Memories from my childhood came rushing to my head, also uninvited like the officer's touch, and I told myself it wasn't like before, even though everything around me seemed familiar—a small room, darkness, an uninvited hand. She finished the "inspection" and by then shame had taken over me. I was looking down, asking God to help me focus, so when she asked me, "*Cuanto le pagaste al coyote,*" my mind was already scrambling for answers to questions I couldn't comprehend, because my mind was lost in another time, many years ago. I kept my head down and I said "*Nada*" and, once again, I felt a familiar twist in my stomach when she said "*Mentirosa, cuanto pagaste?*" I was trembling then. I had just been touched on every part of my body, every single orifice thoroughly inspected by hands that hated me, and now I was being called a liar. But I knew that ICE had already made up their mind about my humanity and its worth even before I came through their door so I didn't feel the need to defend myself. The woman then referred to another female officer who had just walked in and told her, in English, "Look at this little bitch. She is scared now. Bitch should have been scared before she left her shithole home today." And then laughed. I was pretending to only speak Spanish, so I kept my eyes down and didn't say anything. The officer once again said, "*Que me digas, cuanto pagaste?*" to which I responded "*Yo entre con visa.*" She, of course, knew this because, by then, I had already been fingerprinted twice and I saw that my visa came up on their screen. It was clear to me that the whole ten-minute episode was unnecessary and had been carried out to set the tone, mainly for their amusement and to put me in my place. It was part of their duty to their country to make sure people like me knew that we weren't supposed to live at peace in this land. I thought about what she said, that I should have been scared before I left my home and I thought how true that must have been for the women I was going to meet when I was transferred to the detention center and that ignited my anger. Hours went by. I was very cold and lonely and by then something had cracked in me, something that I had fought to keep together for many years. This was the first layer.

Fear of Failure

> *"Mujeres, a no dejar que el peligro del viaje y la inmensidad del territorio nos asuste—a mirar hacia adelante y a abrir paso en el monte."*

> "Women, let's not let the danger of the journey and the vastness of the territory scare us—let's look forward and open paths in the woods."
> —Cheríe Moraga and Gloria Anzaldúa, *This Bridge Called My Back*

The night I was detained I was sent to a county jail just after midnight. The jail was small and the officers who worked there didn't speak Spanish so I couldn't ask any questions about where I was going. When I got to the jail I saw many small cells, most of them in a row. All of my belongings had been taken. I was only allowed to keep my shirt and my pants. I was shackled from the waist to my wrists and my feet. It was nearly impossible to walk. I was transferred to the small jail with two men and, the moment I tried to talk with them, the officer told me to shut up. I wanted to know desperately where I was going because from what I had been told, the detention center was at least an hour away, but they talked on their radios of arriving in twenty minutes. Once we arrived I realized that the cells were individual and they were completely sealed, except for a window that oversaw the hallway. I hate the dark and I hate being alone. I freaked out. Michigan is not like other states where ICE contracts with private companies to build immigrant-only jails and detention centers. In Michigan, ICE contracts with already existing county jails and allocates a certain number of beds to house immigrants, and for that reason, I wasn't sure that the jail where they took me was my final destination.

We strategically picked Michigan for the infiltration because months earlier, a woman named Janelle who had been detained there tried to commit suicide twice. And when activists asked for her release in order that she receive mental health treatment, ICE Michigan deported her immediately. ICE Michigan's recklessness and known cruelty made the state a perfect, but also a very scary, target.

My stomach hurt; I hadn't eaten anything except for a small juice and a piece of bread I was given after five hours of questioning. I tried to make a phone call to the group outside who was waiting for news but the phone was not working. Someone came knocking at my door and said in English "Go to sleep, we are taking a little trip in a few hours." I figured that meant I was probably being transferred to the jail in Battle Creek, Michigan, where we knew most undocumented immigrants were held. I tried calling over and over again and minutes later I was able to connect with the group outside. The initial plan was for myself and another woman to be detained together as to make our job inside easier if we found a large number of detainees. But the group informed me that the other woman had not been detained after officers found out she had applied for DACA, and that she was going to try to get detained again the morning.

After I hung up, I tried to sleep but I could not because too many thoughts raced through my head. What if I can't gain the trust of the women? What if they think I am crazy and trying to get them in trouble? What if they don't want to fight back? Up until then, I had read enough Zora Neale Hurston and James Baldwin to know that I couldn't save anybody and to know that the women did not have to trust me. Why would they? They did not know me. All my ideas about power and organizing would not matter to them or anybody else inside unless I first worked on building relationships with them, and that these relationships couldn't solely be based on our lack of immigration status. I kept thinking of an answer to give them if they asked why I was saying I could help with their release if I couldn't even help with my own release. Of course I came in with my own insecurities and romanticized revolutionary ideals, but

I also knew that I knew the system, and that the best release organizing campaign I ever worked on was that of my nephew. I reminded myself that I had decided to infiltrate mainly because I thought any of those women could be one of my sisters any given day. I should have known then that most of these things I was worried about would not matter to these women the moment we opened up with each other about other aspects of our lives.

Hours went by, and finally an officer came to take me out. He asked if I knew English because he needed help translating and I immediately said "yes." He first shackled me around the waist and then around my feet and my hands. By the time I got to the lobby, I saw that five Latino men were already there wearing blue uniforms, two of them were crying. The officer told me to tell them that we were all being transferred to a jail in Calhoun County where we were going to speak with immigration officers and see a judge to then be deported. I knew the deportation part didn't have to be true and I knew the officers didn't speak Spanish so I translated that we were being transferred to a similar jail in a different county where they were going to have a chance to fight their cases. One man began to ask if he could inform his family of the transfer, but as I translated, the officer told me he couldn't answer questions, that once we got to Calhoun, we could figure it out. I apologized to the man and told him that the officer didn't want to answer questions and he began to sob even more. Translating for ICE reminded me of when I worked in the restaurant industry and the managers asked me to translate to the table bussers and dishwashers. Often, they wanted me to tell them to work faster or tell them that their hours were being cut. In those settings, with "authority or power figures," I was forced to use my native tongue to translate oppressive language and it made me angry. I wanted to use my Spanish to comfort the sobbing man or to explain that I had a number they could call where they may be able to get some help, but I was silenced once again, my mother tongue mocked and shamed.

The men and I were loaded in the truck and taken to Calhoun County Jail. On the way there, I tried to distract the ICE officers so I could pass money and a phone number to the other detainees. We stopped to get gas and I saw that one of the officers was coming back with a Dr. Pepper. I got close to the window (they sat me in the first row in case they needed me to translate again) and told the officer, "Do you know Dr. Pepper is made in Texas and has twenty-three flavors?" He turned around and said "Is that right? How do you know English? How long have you been in America?" I said, "Thirteen years" to which he responded, "You must have done something really bad for us to deport you." The truth is, neither I, nor the men inside the van, nor anyone else had done anything that justified a deportation. But it was useless to have that conversation with the officers so as he went back outside the van, I managed to pass around a phone number and some money, and tell the men why I was there. I don't know what happened to any of those men.

I got to the detention center and, after being separated from the men, I was processed for a while, this included another thorough strip search. I was then given an orange uniform and sent to my cell. Because this was a county jail and not an immigration-only facility, I was detained with what is normally referred to as "the general population," meaning U.S. citizens and residents who were there for non-immigration related charges. As soon as I got to my cell, my cellmate introduced herself and told me that I had arrived at a bad time because lunch had just passed and we wouldn't be fed again until 4 a.m. I told her it was okay and I just wanted to rest. She told me that there was no such a thing as rest in this place. She asked what my name was and what I had done. I told her my name was Claudia and I hadn't necessarily done anything. I just got caught without papers. She said, in a warm tone, that she wasn't there to judge me and that I could tell her what I had done openly. I insisted I hadn't done anything and tried to explain to her that not having papers in this country could land you in jail. She grew frustrated with me and told me that she found it odd that all of the American (by this she meant black and white) women there were open about their crimes, but that all that the Latinas did was cry a lot and say they hadn't done anything. She left the room and I tried to sleep.

I woke up and went outside for recess and sat with a woman who also asked me about what I had done. I told her that I had come to this country illegally. She accepted this answer so I then asked her what she had done. She told me that she got charged with lying about a crime, but that she hadn't done it. She said that she found out a local police officer had tried to rape her teenage daughter and when she went to report him and the officer found out, he went to her house while she wasn't there and made her daughter, under duress and threats, sign a paper recanting her story. Her daughter was scared that the cop might try to hurt her mom, who had been previously arrested on prostitution and drug charges and who was now on probation, so she signed the paper. What the cop didn't tell her was that once she signed the declaration recanting her story, he was going to file charges against her for "fabricating the story." When her mother (the woman with whom I was speaking) found out what happened, she knew it was going to be nearly impossible to fight the cops without a good lawyer in such a small town, which she couldn't afford. So she decided the next best thing she could do was take the blame to make sure her daughter didn't get sent to juvenile detention, so she got arrested and sentenced to seven months in county jail.

When I decided to infiltrate a detention center, I knew that I was going in there to speak with the undocumented women who were victims of a vicious and unjust immigration system, but once I talked to this and other U.S.-citizen women, I realized that as women, we are all pretty much screwed by this country's misogynist and punishment institutions. That night, I tried to sleep in the cell, but I kept thinking about what my cellmate said when I arrived, "There is no rest in this place." I knew she didn't mean physical rest because I could see that she had fallen asleep, but her words made me wonder how many painful secrets, how many tears, how many crushed souls those jail walls held, and how my own life would be changed there. For sure, nothing good could come out of such a dark place.

"All that you touch you Change. All that you Change Changes you. The only lasting truth is Change."
                        —Octavia Butler, *Parable of the Sower*

The urgency for me at the moment was that I was undocumented, that's all I thought about, until the women helped me to see more clearly because they were open and honest about the fact that, for them, it isn't the worst thing that has happened—so you need to get the layers, to understand the layers of pain that have brought these women here. My cellmate asked me to sit with her during breakfast. She told me she could see that I was very young and scared. She wanted to comfort me, telling me she had been there twice and knew everyone's business. She told me who the guards were and gave me a breakdown of all the cells and told me about the people detained there. She said that once the nice guards found out I knew English, they were probably going to ask me to translate for them. She told me that there were about fifteen women there who didn't speak English—about twelve from Mexico (really Latin America, but she thought they were all from Mexico), two from Europe, and one from Asia. She said that one of the Mexican women had gotten sick two days before, but that, since no one could really understand what was happening and the guard on-duty was extremely mean, all they could gather from some of the words she said was that she was diabetic. She said she rushed to her room as this lady almost fainted and brought her a mint she had gotten from commissary the week before. The lady grabbed it quickly and chewed on it, but she continued feeling sick. She told me that maybe I could talk with her if she came out for lunch and told me that most of the Mexican women did not come out for breakfast.

During lunch, I quickly noticed the table with about ten Latina women. I grabbed my lunch and went over to ask if I could sit down. All the women seemed much older than I was and at least half of them seemed withdrawn. One of them was crying. The older lady, Maria, asked my name and how old I was. I told her my name was Claudia and I was in my late twenties. She said I must be around her daughter's age and asked me how I had been detained. I told her that I made a wrong turn at the Canada Bridge. I could quickly tell that Maria was the mother figure to all the other detainees. She told me she had been detained for about four months and that she was probably going to be deported soon because she took blame for a crime her son had committed and that the only reason she was still there was because the judge had given her a chance to find an attorney. But she said her son was also in jail and, with no help on the outside, she would surely be deported. My cellmate came over and told me that Maria was the woman with diabetes about whom she told me earlier. When the women saw that I spoke English, they all stared at me. Maria asked me if I had gone to school here and I said, I did. She then asked me if I had committed a crime because she didn't think that someone who went to school here and was young like me could be deported.

I couldn't lie to Maria and, as all the women were curious about my answer, I told them that I was kind of one of those people they talked about and referred to as "DREAMers." Before I could continue, another woman, Elda, quickly jumped in and said that months earlier she had heard on the news about DREAMers who turned themselves in to infiltrate a detention center in Florida to help people from the inside and she asked if I was with them.[3] I told her that my partner was one of those two people and that yes, I was there for the same purpose. Elda said she wanted to be part of whatever we had planned and the other women agreed with her, though some of them were, understandably, skeptical. After lunch finished, we agreed to meet for dinner so we could discuss our stories and see how to move forward.

That same day, the facility was placed in lock down after a black woman tried to

---

3.   Michael May, "Los Infiltradores," *The American Prospect* (June 21, 2013), accessed January 10, 2016 http://prospect.org/article/los-infiltradores.

commit suicide by using her bed sheets to hang herself from the second floor. There-fore, all detainees had to remain in their cells for the rest of the day. The woman was caught before she could hurt herself but we could hear her screaming and crying. I asked my cellmate what would happen to her and she said that many people attempt suicide and that if you fail, the guards strip you naked and send you to solitary confine-ment for days until they believe you won't hurt yourself anymore. I also felt angry that the woman was mocked by the guards when we were able to go outside the next day and we were told of what would happen if we tried anything "stupid." I asked my cellmate if therapy was available but she chuckled and said it was a joke so nobody went.

Alycia

"Their eyes were all around, one closes and the other three open & when it darkens one can hear noise like cloaked steps without rustle and all the while the Orchids and Hy-drangeas wither between flowerpots without water, without anyone to water them—they dry without hope of flowering the coming days."
—Alycia, *How Flowers Died*[4]

Every night I would go to sleep hearing the cries of mothers missing their children. Only two of the women detained here had no children of their own. Everyone else had at least one child at home awaiting her return. One woman cried for nearly four days and nights without stopping. It was the kind of cry I will never forget in my life. It was so hopeless, so full of pain. It was this woman who made me question my allegiance to any country or citizenship. Mexico had failed her, and now the United States was too. Why would I want to call either place home?

4. Personal field notes.

During lunch, I figured out that most women hadn't heard about their cases or their courts so I helped them fill out forms that were only in English to request that someone inform them of the status of their case. I also talked more to Maria about her medical condition, diabetes, and helped her fill out a medical request form to see a doctor. Then a woman by the name of Alycia got close to the table and told me she had to talk to me in private. During dinner, I sat with Alycia, whose eyes were extremely red and swollen. In broken Spanish, she told me that she wanted to join the group but that she didn't think her husband would allow her. She said that she had three young children, all born in the United States and that her husband told her that she shouldn't fight her case and just wait to get deported because he wanted her to raise the children in Guatemala where she was from. It was then that the complexity of seeing documentation as *the* problem for detained women hit me like a bucket of cold water. What was I suppose to tell Alycia? My thoughts were, what a jerk, screw him, and let's just do it behind his back. But I knew I couldn't tell Alycia all those things without first understanding her situation fully. Over the next two days I spent a lot of time speaking with her. Every time she broke down and every day she changed her mind about creating a campaign. Alycia asked me to have the group outside call her husband and explain the situation, but her husband coldly told my group that he had already planned Alycia's move to Guatemala with the children and that he was not interested in doing anything else.

When I told Alycia what he said, she broke down and told me she couldn't go back to Guatemala. I asked her what happened there and she then began to tell her story, which haunts me to this day. Alycia told me that she was from an indigenous community in Guatemala and that, when she was about six years old, she had to go to the mountains because her parents were part of an indigenous resistance group and they were being persecuted. She said she had to learn how to fight and she was always aware that if they were captured, they were probably going to be killed. But her parents were proud people and she stayed with them. She spent about six years in the mountains and when she was around thirteen years old, she was sent to the city so she could attend school.

While in the city, she was raped by a relative who then threatened to tell the authorities the location of her parents if she did not keep quiet. Alycia kept quiet and endured abuse at the hands of her relative for months until she met another man when she was fifteen years old. Alycia told me she fell in love with this man who was older than her and promised to take her away from the abusive environment in which she lived. And he did, for a year or so until Alycia found out she was pregnant. Alycia's partner told her that he did not want a baby and forced Alycia to have an abortion. Months passed before Alycia decided to come to the United States to see if she could find better luck here. She met her current husband, who she said was nice but a macho who thought she had to do as he said. And with him she had three children, the youngest one a little girl whom now Alycia had to bring with her to Guatemala, a place that terrified Alycia and a place where she thought her daughter could have the same fate she did. When Alycia finished telling me her story, I wept with her. So much pain and trauma had been imposed on this young woman at such a young age. She told me that she attended a very conservative church and that she sometimes felt uneasy about the submissive role that women were told to play in church, but affirmed that Jesus was her only salvation and the light of her life.

I could feel Alycia's faith in a way I can't describe. She prayed for me every night with an intensity and an honesty that I felt deep in my soul. I am not the most religious person, but I am a person of deep faith and deep love, and I could feel both things coming from Alycia. I told her that if she wanted to fight her case, we could put out a petition and bring attention to her case, but she told me to wait.

The next day, I opened up to Alycia about my own story of abuse. This is when we first talked about the many layers of pain we carried with us and when I felt more free because of her honesty. Until then, I hadn't talked to anyone about what happened to me—my layers—and Alycia saved me from keeping it to myself forever. She saved me in ways I could have never saved her. So many layers in our lives—abuse, rape, manipulation, violence, poverty, machismo, illegality.

The day that Alycia was deported (twelfth day of my detention), my heart broke into pieces. They came to take her away at 6 a.m. She gave me a tight hug and told me I could have her food. She said she was always going to remember us and pray for us and she asked us to do the same. I couldn't talk because of my tears, of anger, of fear, of impotence, and complete outrage that became too overwhelming. Alycia touched my face gently. Her last words to me were that at least she was going to be physically free now. Many of the women who I met while in detention remained detained when I left. I was given a $4,000 bond and by the nineteenth day I came to feel like I had failed most of these women, as only three were able to get out with our help. The stories of these women still haunt me and remind me that this country is breaking and destroying hundreds of thousands of lives.

The day that my friends and I made the infiltration story public, to gather media attention behind some of the cases of the women with whom we were working, the jail isolated me from all the women and sent me to solitary confinement. Solitary confinement was truly horrifying, because all the demons that I had managed to push away in my cell did not go away there. The darkness, the coldness, all the stories I now carried with me, all the women I had met and wasn't going to be able to help, everything haunted me. I didn't see the women again until my bond was paid and I was sent to gather my belongings for release. It was then that I found out one of the women with whom my friends and I were working and whose case had seemed, until then, nearly impossible to win had been released. She had taken a leading role after her case became public, and she inspired the rest of the women to want to fight their cases harder. They rest of the women hugged me and asked me not to forget about their stories. I never will, was my answer. I never will.

Love in Times of Darkness
Truth is, citizenship won't stop our suffering. Citizenship won't stop undocumented women from being physically, mentally, and emotionally abused. Citizenship won't stop

black immigrants from being brutalized by the police. Citizenship won't stop undocumented women from being paid less and being seen as one of the most expandable labor groups in this country. Citizenship won't give me back the past twenty years of separation from my mother. Citizenship won't help Alycia who is now deported and back in a country where she knew much pain and suffering. Citizenship won't help the other women who remain in detention today, especially those in family detention camps and those who are forced to flee their countries due to violence and abuse only to come to this country to find more of the same. How do I know this? Because citizenship has not protected generations of black, indigenous, queer, and trans women in this country and continues to fail them every single day.

What I do know is that granting undocumented women legal status can help in taking away an extra layer of pain from the many they carry in their souls. As activists and organizers, we should not betray these women by solely seeking citizenship as a form of relief for them. We should encourage them to find the stories that they carry in their heart, and be available to them if, and when, they ask for layers of healing. As I learned in the jail, we must stand shoulder to shoulder with American women who are also seeking those layers of healing because this country was not designed for us. As survivors, we must claim our rightful place. That is the only way this country has a chance at ever making peace with itself.

I certainly am a woman of faith and I believe that in a small way, faith is what has saved me and stopped me from taking my own life in the darkest moments of my life when death seemed the only option for escape. But I know that being in relationship and sharing love with others has been my true saving grace, my mother's love, my sisters' love, and my dearest and closest friends' love, who understand and know the many layers of pain that I carry with me and who help me find layers of healing, while dealing with their own layers. I have to be honest when I say that the darkness is still present and that it is only through organizing and being in community, helping each other tear down walls, that I can find some light. And I continue to wrestle with these questions every day, especially when I think of Alycia and the many other women I met at Calhoun County Jail, who touched my life and helped me find my own layers. Is love the only hope? If so, who can access love? What is love to the abused, the raped, the exploited, the manipulated, and the expendable? What is love to she whose humanity has been deemed illegal? What is love in the times of darkness? What does love look like as a renewable resource? Who else is out there fighting for radical love? My only answer right now is that if hate and power built borders and prison walls, then only disciplined, creative, caring, and well-resourced love for each other will bring them all down. It sounds simple, but it is not. As Mariame Kaba teaches us, hope is a discipline. And to find those willing to walk into that discipline with us, we must push against every wrong thing we have been conditioned to think about each other, every single day. That's why we infiltrated that jail.

Last year, in the middle of the Trump zero-tolerance family-separation crisis, I received a Facebook message from a family member of one of the women my friends and I worked with at Calhoun County. She said that her mother had been deported earlier in the year but that she came back and she wanted to fight her case like before and needed help. She said that, just like when she was at Calhoun County Jail, attorneys told her she had a losing case and were not willing to help her, but she knew attorneys weren't the only answer. She is now back with her family here in the United States. It was then that I affirmed my belief that, although I may not see borders and prison walls fall down in my lifetime, I have a role to play in this very present by helping create the necessary conditions for that to be the reality one day. And it will be the reality one day, oh it will be, for the road to abolition of everything that harms us (in this case the layers of pain) is paved by single acts of liberation.

CHAPTER 5

Brothers Crossing Borders

Siempre quise yo estudiar
Y ser alguien en la vida
Ser aquel hijo ejemplar
Orgullo de la familia
Un honor para mi pueblo
Y pa mi patria querida.

Pero de nada ha servido
Haberme yo titulado
Como todos mis colegas
Andamos por todos lados
En busca de un buen trabajo
Y sin poder encontrarlo.

El titulo no es basante

I always wanted to go to college
and be someone in life
to be an exemplary son,
to make my family proud &
to be an honor for my people
and for my beloved country.

But nothing has helped me
By graduating from college
Looking for good work and
Unable to find it
The degree is not enough

Los Tigres Del Norte, "El titulado"

Why We Leave Home

My mother remembers very well the day I left our village in Oaxaca, Mexico, with two of my older brothers to travel to the U.S. It was strange to be saying goodbye to my mother, but it was expected of us. I was just fourteen years old. At the time, I didn't feel too young to be leaving home on such a long and dangerous journey. There was no choice really. The North American Free Trade Agreement (NAFTA) devastated our local economy. Even a meager living for our family was no longer possible.[1] To survive meant that some of us had to migrate to look for paid labor in the U.S., the very country that had created NAFTA. If there had been a choice, I would have never left my home.[2]

My mother tells me it was at dawn on a Wednesday in July of 2005. My four younger siblings were still sleeping. My mother packed the few things I would need to cross the desert—tostadas for food, garlic to protect against a snakebite and alcohol to rub on our blisters. My mother and father gave me and my brothers a blessing before we walked out the house. And just as I got into the car to leave, my mother rushed out to ask a special request of the other adults, "Please do not leave Pedro behind because he is so young. Please take care of him." I was the youngest in the group migrating to the U.S. from my village that day. I wasn't sure when I would see my mother again. No one cried. There was no time for feelings. I'm only now, ten years later, remembering the emotional pain to my mom and to myself.

I didn't realize that to come to the U.S. involved risking my life. I walked through the dangerous Sonoran Desert for one week under the bright and hot sun. During the walk I became numb, I think in part so that I could continue walking through the pain. I know now that too many die on this journey. But what choice do we have? When I finally arrived in Kentucky a week later, I took my shoes off to show my feet to my brothers and

1. Alyshia Gálvez, *Eating NAFTA: Trade, Food Policies, and the Destruction of Mexico* (Berkeley: University of California Press, 2018).

2. Tanya Maria Golash-Boza, *Deported: Immigrant Policing, Disposable Labor, and Global Capitalism* (New York: New York University Press, 2015).

family on the other side of the border. I shocked everyone because my feet were covered with painful blisters. My sister-in-law immediately began caring for my feet. She washed them with warm water and put alcohol on them to stop the possibility of infections.

Leaving our village to look for work was not always necessary for our survival. Our lives began to change dramatically after NAFTA, which promised the American Dream for Mexico but only produced a nightmare.[3] It forced the price of corn and other crops so low that our family could no longer make a living from working on our land. We were forced to leave our families and farmland to find industrial and agricultural jobs in large cities north of Oaxaca, *maquiladoras* at the border, and then further in the U.S. NAFTA promised a stronger economy for Mexico, but it only brought us lower wages, family separation, greater poverty, and violence.

Where I Am From

I was born and raised in San Cristóbal Amatlán, a small village that lies below the Sierra Madre del Sur mountain range in the southern part of Oaxaca, Mexico. I have seven brothers and two sisters. I am in the middle, the fifth child. I cannot even begin to count how many generations of my ancestors have lived and died in this village. I spoke Amatlán Zapotec every day in the community and at home. We learned Spanish in school but did not speak it. My memories as a small child in the village are very happy and included lots of work along with playing soccer in the streets. I remember regularly working in the fields, working alongside my parents and siblings through different seasons planting and harvesting different crops. I also helped a lot around the house. I took care of my younger siblings when my mother got sick or when she had to watch someone who was sick as well. It was my responsibility, in addition to these other tasks related to our way of life, to walk a few hours further up the mountains with our donkeys to collect firewood for our cooking stove. This was the life as a small child that I expected would never change.

3. David Bacon, *The Right to Stay Home: How US Policy Drives Mexican Migration* (Boston: Beacon Press, 2014).

I am from the field,
From ashes and wild life.
The taste burned toast.
The sound of the front house,
From nature and union.
Behind yoke and plow,
From bulls, horses, weaver, rivers and the light of day.
I'm a farmer from corn, beans, and wheat.
I live as the sun rises and sets each day.
The never-ending cycle of work, work, work
Days that melt into each other,
No day unlike yesterday or tomorrow.
I find solace under the mango tree.
Responsibility of a farmer's life,
even as a student.
My days working until I arrive at home
Where we speak Zapotec not Spanish.
Our community is close as family,
One big circle.
If one is ill,
No one is ever alone.
A favor given, it is never demanded back,
it is given *por su propia voluntad*.
The birth of a new child
brings the community together,
to share food to the newborn.
Celebrating as community.
United as family.[4]

4. Cefe Martinez Santiago, untitled and unpublished poem, 2011.

Many things have changed for our family and village when we were forced to look for jobs away from our home. We leave to find work to pay for our survival, and then are soon swept up in believing we need more. We think if we work hard enough that we might get some smaller version of the American Dream back in Mexico when we return. This is the lie we believe. The American Dream is destroying us.

Migrating to Live
Soon after NAFTA went into effect, more and more of the men in our village began to leave their families behind to find work. There are now estimates of up to 500,000

indigenous people from Oaxaca living in the U.S.[5] The length of time my father and older brothers went for work outside of San Cristobal to larger cities within Mexico was at first for just a few months. My oldest brother was the first to leave before finishing high school. He went to a neighboring state to work in a cheese factory. As each year passed, my other two older brothers joined him to work at the same place. I missed my older brothers. I remember one day I was taking care of some goats and I knew my oldest brother would be returning home. So I spent most of the day watching the goats close by the road so that I would not miss him when he came. Each time a car passed by I watched it closely so that I wouldn't miss him. Then another car came and he was in it. I was super excited to see him because he had been gone a long time. Tears came out when I saw him. My brothers would come and go for long periods of time until one day in 2000 when they left forever. Two of my oldest brothers left for the U.S. At that time, I never imagined that I would soon follow to live with my brothers in Kentucky.

While my brothers and I were all born in the same village in Oaxaca, we have all ended up in different places still looking for a way to make a living. After crossing, my brothers went to Merced, California, to work where most of the other men from our village had gone. But soon after arriving the U.S., my oldest brother decided to take a chance to find better work in Kentucky. My oldest brother has never left Kentucky and most likely will never return to Oaxaca to see our parents. He married and has three beautiful children my parents have never seen. There is always the fear of deportation, that one day, he may be forced to leave his new family life because he has no papers.

My second oldest brother came and worked in the U.S. for just a few years. We have all worked mostly in restaurants. He was able to save up a small amount of money to return to Mexico and start his own small jeans-making shop out of his home. His new home is located in a large city in a neighboring state to Oaxaca, a ten-hour journey

---

5. Eric Hershberg and Fred Rosen, "Turning the Tide?" in *Latin America After Neoliberalism: Turning the Tide in the 21st Century*, edited by Eric Hershberg and Fred Rosen (New York: New Press, 2006), 23.

from our village. My third oldest brother also came to Kentucky for only a few years. He has returned to live near by oldest brother making cheese in a factory. There is a growing community of people from my village now living in Puebla City near regular factory work, making it feel like a home away from home. My fourth oldest brother and I arrived together in Kentucky where we worked in one restaurant for ten years. He still talks about returning, but he now has a son born here that he enjoys watching grow up.

Then there is Cefe, my fifth brother, who is just a few years younger than me. He came to the U.S. at even a younger age than me, age twelve. He has moved back and forth between Mexico and the U.S. seeking more than work, but something more like freedom and dignity. The rest of my younger siblings still live in our village in Oaxaca, Mexico. They have to move between San Cristobal and Puebla for brief periods along with my parents. My parents are still unable to make enough money while living in San Cristobal to make ends meet to support my two younger brothers and sister. My family can only afford to keep one of them in school, my youngest brother. The other two have not graduated from high school because they have to work. Everyone in the village has to always work beginning at a very early age. So much has changed since my brothers and I left our village, but at the same time, it seems like nothing has changed. We still are courageously enduring suffering.

The College Graduate

As for me, when I arrived in 2005 at the age of fifteen, my older brothers placed me in high school. I didn't speak any English and only some Spanish, but somehow I quickly adapted and graduated with a high school diploma. I worked in a restaurant on nights and weekends to earn enough money to pay for an Associate degree and eventually earned a B.A. degree in anthropology at the University of Kentucky. I became the "DREAMer," the good immigrant deserving of DACA (Deferred Action for Childhood Arrivals), but my brothers, both older and younger than me, are criminalized and labeled the bad immigrants.

In 2010 I started getting involved in activism to fight for the DREAM Act. I got to travel to Washington, D.C., for rallies and at the time I was so excited thinking I was doing something great. It felt good that people were calling us DREAMers. I was one of the first three people in Kentucky to announce in public that I was undocumented and unafraid. People thought I was brave to fight for immigrant rights. But this isn't the whole truth about why I got involved. To be honest, the reason I got involved is a little selfish. I knew the DREAM act would benefit me greatly. I got so lost in all of it. I soon became disillusioned when I began asking about who was fighting for my brothers and my parents back home in Oaxaca. How would any of this make life better for them? I started to think that if everyone was so focused on fighting for just us DREAMers, who was thinking about the bigger picture? Who was thinking about the future of our families?

But the hardest thing to face and let go of was this lie of the American Dream. It was so tempting to believe that this could save me. My brothers had encouraged it. I was considered lucky to have become a DREAMer. But I was starting to see that the very system that had caused so much suffering for my village and family was the same system offering me a way out. I was told going to college was the best way out of my situation. So I worked hard to get a college degree in order to make more money. Everyone told me this was how I could find freedom and happiness. I believed that. And I still believe you can make money by going to college. But now I wonder at what cost to others will I go to get more money. Who is suffering? And in reality, will making more money end my suffering? It is difficult for me to see that that is the answer.

Now I have DACA. It was carefully crafted for many reasons. It only provides a legal presence, but no lawful status. So my status remains unlawful, but my presence is legal. It doesn't make sense to me, but that is what it is. With that I have a work permit and driver's license. But it doesn't change the suffering of my family living in Oaxaca and it doesn't change much the living situation for me living here. In many ways it is very limited. I would say it provides false hope. I can work for the dream in the U.S. legally, but DACA could end at any time making me deportable once again.

After I earned a college degree, I continued to work odd jobs to make ends meet. It was difficult to start a career as everyone was telling me to do, when I could promise no employer more than the two years that DACA allowed. And further, down in my heart, I wanted to be with my family in Oaxaca. I returned to work at the restaurant I first worked in when I arrived to the U.S. ten years ago. I saw the work conditions that I ignored before, where we were treated as less than human. We were simply cogs in a system, someone there to produce, produce, and produce. Was this what it means to be human? Because of my education I was asked, why are you working here still? Don't you have a college degree? I usually said this was only temporary. But in reality, I didn't see how pursuing some other job would change anything for the better, for me, or for the world. I do recognize that an education and DACA have allowed me access to more opportunities and jobs than my brothers. But it seems to me that these opportunities are not available to all, and the jobs they lead to seem only to produce greater inequality.

I was able to return to my village and family in 2014 for a very brief period because DACA provided the opportunity to travel for educational, employment, and humanitarian purposes. The trip home on a plane was so much shorter and safer than the one that brought me to the U.S. Why do we force people to migrate through dangerous deserts to provide for their families? Everyone was fourteen years older than when I left, so much had changed. My family was so happy to see me and I knew right away it would be hard to leave. I loved participating again in the village festivities, the dancing and music, and eating my mother's food. As I visited with others throughout the village listening to their stories I recognized that so many family members were still missing. Those living here still rely on income made from work outside our village. The stories that were the most difficult to hear while home were those told by my mother and father about what had happened to every family in our community and the ongoing family separation and the struggle to make a living. I had never heard them share these stories before about what had happened to my childhood friends and neighbors, but I already knew what they were telling me because I had lived it too. We shared many tears together. My father asked what he could have done differently. How can I make a satisfying life? My mother apologized for failing to provide for my brothers and me. She blamed herself that we all had to leave home on that dangerous journey north. And then she just said how sad it was to miss her children. I just held her and repeated again and again, it was not your fault. Because it was not their fault!

The Search for Human Dignity and Freedom

My younger brother Cefe took a very different path than all of us. He came to the U.S. after me at an even younger age. He had the same opportunity to graduate from a high school in the U.S., but upon graduation he believed that further education would not make him happy. He had the opportunity to become a DREAMer, but he responded to all of the encouragement to go to college by saying there was no need to. He didn't believe in any of America's good intentions or promises. He didn't want to do anything to change his status because he saw it as a hopeless. He said he was content and just wanted to live a simple life. No one could convince him to go to college. His goals were simple. He just wanted to make a little money and then return to Mexico to work as a farmer in our village.

One year after finishing high school, Cefe decided to go back to our village in Oaxaca because he didn't see a life here, at least one with work that does not destroy one's humanity. He saw how hard my brothers worked for minimum wage while being mistreated and exploited. But upon his return he found that life in Oaxaca was not as he idealized. He left as a child six years earlier. The community was not as close as he remembered in his poem. People returned from the U.S. to build fancier homes where they now lived a different lifestyle and kept more to themselves. And while he loved the hard work of working on the land, his money soon ran out and he could not make a living as a farmer as he hoped.

He was forced once again to leave the village to look for work in Puebla. He was reminded of the suffering that he could not escape on either side of the border. He decided to attempt to cross the desert once again to the U.S. but was caught by border patrol and returned. It was at this time that I contacted him to tell him about the DREAM 9 border action in the summer of 2013 led by the National Immigrant Youth Alliance.[6] Three U.S. Dream Act eligible youth agreed to self-deport to Mexico in order to cross back to the U.S. with six other Dream Act eligible youth who left the U.S. briefly but had encountered difficulties and wanted to return.[7] Cefe was one of them.

Cefe didn't join the action to change anything or fix America, or as he says to become a hero. He supported the messaging of the action, but at the same time he didn't think it would do anything. He really just wanted to return to the U.S. He agreed with the other participants that America's political system, and in particular the politicians advocating for comprehensive immigration reform (CIR) had failed the immigrant community. So Cefe joined eight other undocumented youth from Mexico who had lived much of their lives in the U.S., to walk through the Nogales border check point to confront and challenge President Obama's administration's record of mass deportations including many low priority migrants and DREAMers.

Cefe's life provides a way for me to see things differently. First, he has helped me see activism and civil disobedience from another perspective. I still think that what he and the others accomplished with the DREAM 9 action was important to push against CIR compromises for the few, to fight for the dignity of the larger migrant community. But he reminds me, through the way he lives his life, that on every other ordinary day living in the U.S. as an undocumented person, he is an activist in the struggle to work and live with dignity. Every day, our existence in the U.S. is labeled "illegal." We have to see and celebrate that every one within our community who took the risk to cross the border to find work to provide for their families are activists. They are the real heroes

6. Aura Bogado, "The Dream 9 Come Home," *Colorlines*, August 8, 2013, https://www.colorlines.com/articles/dream-9-come-home.

7. Antonia Cereijido and Marlon Bishop, "The Dream 9," *Latino USA*, October 16, 2015, http://latinousa.org/2015/10/16/1542-the-dream-9.

—our mothers and fathers and brothers and sisters who courageously every day disobey an unjust system to protect their families' right to live.

Cefe has also experienced incredible challenges on both sides of the border looking for meaningful work that provided a living that did not cost his dignity. He never found it and it may not exist. And when we talk about further education as a path to happiness, he has convinced me that it offers little hope. I see with him that the education system really mostly teaches obedience, to fit in and accept things as they are. What we need is more disobedience. Cefe teaches me that the reality of the world is so different from what is taught in the classroom. Education teaches you to be a part of system that ignores suffering that exists in the world. And there is not a space or a time to discuss this in the classroom. It is difficult to get classmates, even teachers, to see this reality, because all of their lives they have viewed the world from the perspective of privilege. They have no idea what it means to suffer, to be oppressed. They don't know the working conditions of the people who produce the things they consume.

So that is what Cefe is teaching me. I went through all that education. I obeyed all the rules as best as I could. I became the good immigrant. And I see that. But it hasn't provided any freedom for me or for my family. I miss my home and it is hard to see the way forward. There is a "tumult in my soul," as Freire describes, "along with a guilt feeling at leaving one's world, one's soil, the scent of one's soil, one's folks. To the tumult in the soul belongs the pain of the broken dream, utopia lost. The danger of losing hope."[8]

8. Paulo Freire, *Pedagogy of Hope: Reliving Pedagogy of the Oppressed* (New York: Continuum, 1994), 31.

CHAPTER 6

Acompañando

"*... As long as I love so unconditionally you will be here with me. If I remember this I'll be ok. You can go in peace, I promise I will.*" I can't remember exactly how I found out. My mind was in a fog. It was early and as a new mom, I was suffering from sleep deprivation. I woke up while my baby was still asleep, trying to get ready for the day. I got my phone and looked at my messages. There was a voicemail and something was posted on Shaun's Facebook wall. The message was from Shaun's girlfriend, "We are in the hospital" the voice said. "Shaun wanted me to tell you that he will turn in his draft soon." I was Shaun's graduate adviser. Shaun had been doing action research—a research approach that seeks change—with undocumented youth, we were scheduled to present a paper at a national conference in a few weeks. Thinking about how I was going to accommodate the delay in our schedule, I glanced at his Facebook wall. "Shaun passed away" someone had posted. I thought to myself, "What kind of sick joke is this?" Shaun and his friends had a pretty dark sense of humor. Annoyed I replied, "Can someone tell me what's going on?" To further my annoyance, my phone rang, I wondered who could be calling so early in the morning—would I now have enough time to take a shower before my daughter wakes up? I answered the phone still in a fog and thinking about my day, "Hi, Shaun is..." said a voice that sounded like a mumble. I could not understand and just replied "Oh, ok." "Did you hear what I said, Shaun is dead?" I paused, I could now hear clearly. My heart sank and the world stopped.

I met Shaun when he was an undergraduate student. He was the kind of student a professor recognizes as bright but rough around the edges. He was extremely well read, craved ideas, and had an uncanny ability to connect real-life experiences to the thoughts of scholars whose writing came from a time and place very different from the experiences of a young Chicano veteran from the barrios of Corpus Christi, TX. Shaun exuded *cholo*. His tattoos and low-riding pants sometimes made fellow students and colleagues assume that he was rough, not serious, or not smart. Shaun was anything but; he was serious about ideas and actions to challenge poverty and racism. He pursued these with knowledge, intention, and unwavering commitment. His smile conveyed to all of us who had the privilege to know him a gentleness and ease that comes from someone who feels proud about his path.

Shaun was a proud Chicano and he shared his pride in many ways, including in his commitment to give others the opportunity of an education. He was committed to school and to his future as a scholar activist. He hardly ever looked back and barely talked about his past in the barrio and in the military, except to say that it gave him the foundation to be proud of his Mexican roots. As a young Latino from the barrio, Shaun drew on this experience to inspire others. His body, marked by the color of his skin and artful tattoos, displayed his sense of belonging to a heritage that he felt proud of and that he cherished for the wisdom it provided to fight back. For Shaun, college was about resistance, "One of the biggest things I came to college for was to challenge the dominant ideology that you have to eat with this fork or that you have to dress like this. I'm here just to say no you don't. I can be professional in my Dickies and a cutoff shirt. I'm here just to show that you don't have to conform just to succeed."

I was not surprised when Shaun became interested in graduate school and when he applied and got accepted to the Master's program where I teach. As a graduate student, Shaun's applied research involved working with a Texas undocumented, youth-led group by focusing on their educational experiences.[1] He contributed to raise awareness

---

1. Mariela Nuñez-Janes and Shaun Chapa, "'Do I look Illegal?' Undocumented Latino Students and the Challenges of Life in the Shadows," in *The Education of the Hispanic Population*, edited by Billie Gastic and Richard R. Verdugo (Charlotte: Information Age Publishing, 2013), 99–117.

about the DREAM Act by accompanying youth in acts of civil disobedience, supporting their educational campaigns, and sharing his talents as a DJ. Shaun blossomed intellectually and emotionally during his work with undocumented youth. Intellectually he was able to combine his passion for education, philosophy, and Chicanismo. In the undocumented youth movement, Shaun was able to find *La Causa. La Causa*, or "the cause," was utilized by the Chicano civil rights movement to refer to multiple struggles against oppression and collective actions towards liberation among Mexican-Americans. Shaun was deeply aware of this history and its implications for contemporary struggles. The entertainment show *Ardillando*, on the North Texas TV channel, featured a special Spanish-language report on Shaun.[2] He is described as knowing how to *"prender la fiesta"* (start a party) and as a *"leader y visionario"* (leader and visionary). In the show, he discussed the intersections he saw between the experiences of undocumented youth and U.S. citizens raised in the barrio: "One of the biggest reasons I feel so close to them is because, growing up, I kind of felt like them, they don't feel accepted." Shaun explained the rejection he experienced from the wider community, even after his service in the Marines. Although he was proud of this service, Shaun often explained that he dismissed the stereotyping and discrimination, "accepting," as he put it, "a lot of what they did to me." Like the undocumented youth that became his *familia,* Shaun recognized that the oppressions and dreams of Latinx people are multidimensional. The solutions to these multiple and intersectional oppressions are not solved by the state bestowing "rights," but through the fight for universal humanity and *dignidad.*

Emotionally Shaun was able to find *compañerismo* (camaraderie), a community that he regarded as his *familia* among undocumented youth activists and allies. Here, he found unconditional love. His work with undocumented youth made him a better father to his young daughter. The sacrifices he made allowed him to lead by example, as he would put it, by showing the need to fight for what is right and prioritize education.

2.   The show can be seen on YouTube at https://www.youtube.com/watch?v=dNLBgaGtoRA (undated), accessed September 25, 2019.

I did not know about some of these sacrifices until his passing. Shaun used to sleep in his car when he would travel to Corpus Christi to visit his daughter. Here, Shaun would read and write into the night. He would do this to stay awake and to meet many of the deadlines I would set for our research together. He never complained and never asked for any kind of accommodations.

The Dream is Dead

During the last days of his life, Shaun's biggest concern was his school work. When he passed away, I was asked to speak about him at several events organized by students, activists, and family. It was also my role to initiate the administrative tasks needed to make sure the university would recognize his efforts and award his Master's degree posthumously. Shaun's death spread in social media and was widely documented in various university and local news outlets. I delivered an homage to him during my university's first Raza Graduation, an event that he worked tirelessly for and that crystalized his vision. Raza Graduation is part of a long tradition of commencement events put together by Chicano students to honor their families and cultures as significant to their academic achievements. During this event, Shaun's friends staged an entrance into the celebration that evoked the rallies and acts of civil disobedience that Shaun had been a part of as he accompanied undocumented youth. I prepared a short talk about Shaun's legacy that was almost incomprehensible to the audience. In front of a large audience, the fatigue of holding back my emotions took over in the form of unstoppable tears. I could tell my colleagues in the audience felt uncomfortable. I could read their piercing eyes and minds. I did not rise to the occasion of graduation speaker, what an embarrassment. I was left alone to struggle with my emotions in public. In that moment, after witnessing his friends march into Raza Graduation, after seeing and living Shaun's dream without him, I felt Shaun's death as the loss of the promise of education.

Shaun's passing had resulted from being overcome by pneumonia. In the weeks prior to his death, he was ill with what he called a terrible cold. Yet he continued working hard trying to make ends meet and writing papers. Shaun went to the emergency room only after he completed a gig as a DJ, even though he was visibly sick. He worked to death. His education did nothing to protect him. I felt guilty. I promised Shaun that furthering his education would lead him to a better life. Instead of safety, in school, Shaun struggled to survive against the odds caused by his vulnerabilities as a first generation Latino graduate student. I could not help but mourn Shaun's death as the death of a dream.

I realized that, in what initially felt like a moment of shame, in other people's minds, there was no room for grieving in my role as a professor and mentor. I kept thinking about the overwhelming feeling of fulfillment I felt as colleagues organized an altar for Shaun during a scholarly presentation we were scheduled to be a part of and that took place before Raza Graduation. Here, I read Shaun's research, his work with undocumented youth, on his behalf, accompanied by his image, his words, his thoughts and embraced by the tradition of honoring and celebrating the dead. I felt *acompañada* (accompanied) in my grief for the first time and I felt *acompañada* intellectually as I heard Enrique Sepúlveda talk about *acompañamiento* as it related to his work with teachers of undocumented youth.[3] While I was reading Shaun's work a slight breeze was felt in the large ballroom, the lights flickered, and we could all feel his presence. It was in this moment that the borders that demarcate my multiple roles and that dissociated me from feeling grief and engaging the humanity of Shaun's death dissipated. I felt liberated by entering this third space in which I allowed myself to feel my student's humanity and to be embraced by others as fully human in an academic space.

Siempre en la lucha: A Community Biography of Shaun Chapa is the title of a book envisioned by the Chapa Collective. The collective thought of fourteen chapters to document the multiple facets, struggles, and triumphs of someone we collectively knew and loved in different ways. The conclusion is entitled "Lo que sigue" (what comes after)

3. Enrique Sepúlveda III, "Toward a Pedagogy of Acompañamiento: Mexican Migrant Youth Writing from the Underside of Modernity," *Harvard Educational Review* 81 (Fall 2011): 550–73.

because, despite the various ways through which we came to know Shaun and the different aspects about him that we knew, we collectively recognized that Shaun lives, he continues to exist, in our collective struggle for liberation. *Lo que sigue* after death is the light we find in honoring those who paved the way so that we may find light in the darkness.

To feel for others and for oneself are important to liberation. I allowed myself to think about grief and feel grief as a professor. To do so helped me access our common humanity and it required that I tapped into a space of intimacy, often considered an inappropriate space. As a professor, I became accustomed to practices that I intellectually critiqued. Patrolling the lines of the personal/professional, keeping a distance from students' real lives are ways through which the corporatization of educational spaces make their mark on the lives of students and educators. We become disassociated from each other by standardizing/regulating the ways in which we care for our students. Michele Fine writes about how schools have become border patrols by closing the gates to students through standardized forms of testing and by incorporating practices that require they leave their culture outside of school doors.[4] To grieve for Shaun, I had to accept this kind of intimacy, one that acknowledged all of him, one that stood side by side with his struggle. Even in death, Shaun is my *acompañante*, he taught me how to be an accomplice in the struggle for liberation. Shaun taught me what solidarity looks like in action. He is my teacher and I continue to be his pupil.

Seeking Liberation through Love and *Acompañamiento*

It is ironic that such a fundamental part of our humanity requires so much explanation. As an *acompañante*, Shaun taught me about the urgency to act with love and care. Through his actions in life and death, Shaun showed me how to use love as a tool for action. Through his sacrifices, he taught me about creating the kind of selfless intimacy

---

4. Michele Fine and Reva Jaffe-Walter, "Swimming: On Oxygen, Resistance, and Possibility for Immigrant Youth under Siege," *Anthropology & Education Quarterly* 38, no. 1 (2007): 76–96.

required for caring. Chela Sandoval sees love as a hermeneutic, a methodology of social movements that envision change based on their own understanding of their lived experiences. As Sandoval writes, "it is love that can access and guide our theoretical and political *'movidas'*—revolutionary maneuvers toward decolonized being"[5] Some of Shaun's *movidas* included sleeping in his car so that he could visit his daughter and write his papers for class, fasting as a form of protest so that Cesar Chavez could be included in the curriculum, being the DJ for every Latinx organization that would ask and for national gatherings of undocumented youth, showing up to our special 10:30 a.m. Thursday office hours no matter what, demanding that I name my daughter, Shaunna, to honor the fact that he witnessed my belly grow during office hours, trusting me and others, being a proud Chicano, finding love in struggle.

In Spanish, *cariño* is a word that specifically emphasizes the deep human bonds that are part of love and are sometimes distinct from romantic attachments. To care or be bonded by *cariño* requires that someone teaches *cariño* and someone is the recipient of it. *Cariño* is a process that is experienced through teaching and learning. Because *cariño* is taught and learned through lived experiences, it is an everyday pedagogy. This "communal knowing" is the kind of education I received from Shaun.[6] He used his lived experiences as a way to demand justice for others. By recognizing his Chicano roots and his experiences as a low-income single father Mexicano in the academy, he legitimized his experiential knowledge and he inspired others to follow. One of Shaun's dearest projects was hosting elementary school–aged Latinos at our campus. He particularly emphasized the need for college-aged male Latinos to act as role models. I continue to hear stories from activists of color and former students about how Shaun's mentorship impacted their path. Shaun

5. Chela Sandoval, *Methodology of the Oppressed* (Minneapolis: University of Minnesota Press, 2000), 140.
6. Francisca E. Godinez, Dolores Delgado Bernal, and Sofia Villenas, eds., *Chicana/Latina Education in Everyday Life: Feminista Perspectives on Pedagogy and Epistemology* (Albany: State University of New York Press, 2006), 2.

showed them the importance of *educación, testimonios, sobrevivir*, or *convivir*. Through his everyday pedagogy, I was able to see how we, as Latinos, immigrants, and marginalized communities access different starting points, as Bernal suggests, to conceptually and practically envision coalition building and address injustice.[7] Through his mentorship, I learned about the need to decenter other people's ideas, academic ideas, and center lived experiences as a way to enter the conversation about undocumented migration in solidarity. From this lived space filled with contradictions, emotions, and untapped knowledge, I learned to acknowledge pain as part of redemption and I forgave the parents of undocumented youth, and my parents, *por las decisiones en que no fuimos consultados*.

Like Shaun, those of us who are willing to recognize and inhabit this space where both shadow and light collide call ourselves *acompañantes*. *Acompañamiento*, in this sense, can be an important way to learn how to live through and move beyond the shadows of injustice. In the collective action intrinsic to the act of accompaniment, we dismantle the nightmare. In this journey towards freedom, undocumented youth often find allies who, like me, profess to help or advocate. But the term and the practice of being an ally often falls short of creating the necessary conditions for love and *cariño* to flourish. Marco Galaviz, drawing on the work of Jeff Duncan-Andrade, identifies different types of allies in the undocumented youth movement.[8] A "wanksta" is an ally who, as he describes it, talks the talk, but, "when it comes down to doing the hard work and actually supporting a movement or a group of people, they bail or are too busy or don't actually do anything." A "gangsta" is an ally who is in a movement for selfish motives, like self-recognition or money. A "rida" is "someone who is willing to take a bullet for the people they serve. They practice a praxis of *cariño* in all aspects of the work.... It means belonging and living with the community you claim to work for. Similarly, in

---

7. Ibid.
8. Marco Galaviz, "Gangsta, Wanksta, Rida: Allies in the Undocumented Youth Movement," Dream Team @ NYU website, September 19. 2013, https://nyudreamteam.wordpress.com/2013/09/19/gangsta-wanksta-rida-allies-in-the-undocumented-youth-movement.

their discussion of Black Lives Matter, Petersen-Smith and Bean discuss various forms of ally-ship.[9] Allies' roles are to passively support Black activists, or to use their privilege to dismantle racism. As they suggest, in these forms of ally-ship, the relationship between Black and whites, in this particular case, is limited to the role of supported or supporter. Furthermore, this relationship, they suggest, is limited by a focus on interpersonal dynamics and as such does not integrate the historical and structural mechanisms that create racism. Thus, what these forms of ally-ship lack is an emphasis on activism—"activity to challenge racism beyond the self."

This emphasis of working with/in action was a central feature of Shaun's *acompañamiento*—a displacement of the self and an emphasis on community as the focus of activity. *Acompañamiento* finds company in synonyms like "communion" and "solidarity," words that themselves come from the historical struggles of working Black, indigenous, and Latin American peoples. According to Jordi Planella, "Acompañamiento" is a pluridimensional pedagogy involving the mind, body, and spirit; it is also a word that signals the teaching and learning practices of Latino/a migrant families in the U.S.[10] As such, it carves a space for connecting migrant struggles with struggles against racism, sexism, homophobia, and for self-determination. To *acompañar* means to acknowledge the forces of capitalism and power that prevent migrant families from living and working in dignity, and to be in solidarity with multiple struggles for freedom. Shaun did not die alone: he was accompanied by the people who loved him, his love for his daughter, his quest for a better future, and his dream of justice. In death, he was surrounded by hundreds of people who came together to my campus for a beautiful candlelight vigil to commemorate his legacy. He was in the company of strangers who paid their respects on social media, at conferences, and at informal gatherings. He was accompanied by

9. Khury Petersen-Smith and Brian Bean, "Fighting racism and the limits of 'ally-ship,'" SocialistWorker.org, May 14, 2015, http://socialistworker.org/2015/05/14/fighting-racism-and-the-limits-of-allyship.

10. Jordi Planella, "Educación social, acompañamiento y vulnerabilidad: hacia una antropología de la convivencia," *Revista Iberoamericana de Educación* 46 (2008), 5–25.

students who dedicated the first Raza Graduation at my university in his honor. To bring people together was his vision, to accompany his legacy is my responsibility. I just wish he were alive to see it. I wish he did not have to die for us to realize the urgent need to accompany those in struggle. Chapatista forever, siempre en la lucha!

Image Captions for Photos

Page 40: Mixed-media art collaboration (Marco Saavedra and Stephen Pavey, 2012). First direct action with civil disobedience led by undocumented youth of the National Immigrant Youth Alliance after the failure of the DREAM Act to pass in December 2010. (Atlanta, GA, 2011)

Page 41: First direct action with civil disobedience led by undocumented youth of the National Immigrant Youth Alliance after the failure of the DREAM Act to pass in December 2010. Georgia banned undocumented students from attending any public colleges or universities in the state. (Atlanta, GA, 2011)

Page 42: Undocumented youth-led direct action in front of the Supreme Court after the mock "Dream Graduation" nearby. (Washington, D.C., June 2012)

Page 43: Direct action with six undocumented youth arrested for civil disobedience with several youth under the age of eighteen participating. (Atlanta, GA, June 2011)

Page 44: Direct action that included civil disobedience by both undocumented youth and their undocumented parents. (Montgomery, AL, November 2011)

Page 45: Preparing for civil disobedience and direct action. (Indianapolis, IN, May 2011)

Page 46 (left): Direct action and civil disobedience in the Indiana Governor's office. (Indianapolis, IN)

Page 46 (right): May Day direct action and civil disobedience by undocumented youth. (Portland, OR, May 2012)

Page 47: Sit-in and direct action pushing the Obama administration to pass Deferred Action for Childhood Arrivals (DACA). (Cincinnati, OH, June 2012)

Page 48: Immigrant women and allies walked a hundred miles to Pope Francis visiting the U.S. to advocate for migrant justice. (Washington, DC, September 2015)

Page 50: Painting of James Baldwin by Marco Saavedra (2012)

Page 51: Painting of James Baldwin by Marco Saavedra (2012)

Page 52: Direct Action part of the larger infiltration of Broward Detention Center by two undocumented youth. (Pompano Beach, FL, August 2012)

Page 53 (top): Direct Action part of the larger infiltration of Broward Detention Center by two undocumented youth. (Pompano Beach, FL, August 2012)

Page 53 (bottom): Direct Action part of the larger infiltration of Broward Detention Center by two undocumented youth. (Pompano Beach, FL, August 2012)

Page 54: DREAM9 direct action led by National Immigrant Youth Alliance. (Nogales, Sonora, Mexico, July 2013)

Page 55: DREAM9 direct action led by National Immigrant Youth Alliance. (Nogales, Sonora, Mexico, July 2013)

Page 56: BRINGTHEMHOME direct action with DREAM34 led by National Immigrant Youth Alliance. (Nuevo Laredo, Mexico, September 2013)

Page 57: BRINGTHEMHOME direct action with DREAM34 led by National Immigrant Youth Alliance. (Nuevo Laredo, Mexico, September 2013)

Page 58 (left): BRINGTHEMHOME direct action at Otay border crossing led by National Immigrant Youth Alliance to reunite 150 deported individuals with their families in the U.S. (Tijuana, Mexico, March 2014)

Page 58 (right): BRINGTHEMHOME direct action at Otay border crossing led by National Immigrant Youth Alliance to reunite 150 deported individuals with their families in the U.S. (Tijuana, Mexico, March 2014)

Page 59: BRINGTHEMHOME direct action at Otay border crossing led by National Immigrant Youth Alliance to reunite 150 deported individuals with their families in the US. (Tijuana, Mexico, March 2014)

Page 60 (left): Civil Disobedience advocating for #NOT1MORE deportation. (Washington, D.C., August 2014)

Page 60 (right): Direct action at SOA Watch Vigil advocating to shut down Steward Detention Center. (Lumpkin, GA, November 2011)

Page 61: Direct action and civil disobedience blocking a bus of undocumented immigrants headed to the nearby airport for deportation. (Chicago, IL, November 2013)

Page 62 (left): Civil disobedience blocking ICE Detention Center road access to advocate for #NOT1MORE detention or deportation. (Atlanta, GA, September 2016)

Page 62 (right): Civil disobedience blocking ICE Detention Center road access to advocate for #NOT-1MORE detention or deportation. (Atlanta, GA, September 2016)

Page 63 (top): March and direct actions led by Mijente at the Democratic National Convention. (Philadelphia, PA, July 2016)

Page 63 (bottom): March and direct actions led by Mijente at the Republican National Convention. (Cleveland, OH, July 2016)

Page 64 (top): Rally and march led by Mijente in support of expanding sanctuary to protect immigrants from deportations and to defy Trump. (Philadelphia, PA, March 2017)

Page 64 (bottom): Rally and march led by Mijente in support of expanding sanctuary to protect immigrants from deportations and to defy Trump. (Philadelphia, PA, March 2017)

Page 65: Rally and direct action led by Juntos to close down Berks immigrant detention center. (Berks, PA, July 2015)

Page 66: Civil disobedience and Presente vigil led by SOA Watch. (Nogales, AZ, November 2018)

Page 68: Left: Marco arrested for civil disobedience outside Broward Detention Center in Pompano Beach, Florida Right: Marco as a small child in Oaxaca just before migrating to the US with his parents

Page 84: Unnamed "DREAMer" in 8th or 9th grade in U.S.

Page 100: Claudia Muñoz, infiltration of Calhoun County Correctional Center, Michigan, 2013

Page 120: Top: Pedro with his Brothers in Kentucky Bottom: Pedro's parents

Page 125: Pedro's village in Oaxaca

Page 134: Top left: Shaun the DJ Top right: Mariela (professor) speaking at a rally for asylum seekers, Denton, TX Bottom left: Shaun and Mariela attending a Chicano/a Studies conference, Dallas, TX Bottom right: Shaun with the love of his life, his daughter

CONTRIBUTORS

Claudia Muñoz is a graduate of Prairie View A&M University. She lives in Austin, Texas, where she works with Grassroots Leadership to end the criminalization, detention, and deportation of immigrants.

Mariela Nuñez-Janes, PhD, is an Associate Professor of Anthropology at University of North Texas. For more than a decade she has worked with undocumented youth and migrant families as a scholar activist publishing collaborative articles and book chapters on Latino/a education, youth activism, and feminist pedagogies and supporting their journeys in schools and universities.

Stephen Pavey, PhD, is an anthropologist and photographer at Hope in Focus. His scholarship and activism with undocumented youth has grown through intersectional solidarity building to include activist photography with indigenous and people of color led movements for Black Lives Matters, Not 1 More Deportation, Free Palestine, and Mni Wiconi, among other efforts to challenge state violence, mass incarceration, militarization of the police, and the securitization of borders.

Fidel Castro Rodriguez is an undocumented immigrant living in the shadows despite being in the US for almost two decades. He is a graduate of the University of North Texas with degrees in anthropology and French. He works at odd jobs to support himself with hopes to finish his Master's degree in business.

Marco Saavedra is an artist and works at his parent's restaurant in New York City, La Morada. He is co-author of *Shadows Then Light* and *"Make Holy the Bare Life": Theological Reflections on Migration Grounded in Collaboration with Youth Made Illegal by the United States*. The story of his clandestine work in an immigrant detention center is told in the award-winning film *The Infiltrators* (2019).

Pedro Santiago Martinez is a graduate from the University of Kentucky with a degree in anthropology and works as the state-wide recruiter for the Northern Kentucky Migration Education Regional Center. NPR recently covered his community research project, "The Latino Experience in Appalachia."

AK Press is small, in terms of staff and resources, but we also manage to be one of the world's most productive anarchist publishing houses. We publish close to twenty books every year, and distribute thousands of other titles published by like-minded independent presses and projects from around the globe. We're entirely worker-run and democratically managed. We operate without a corporate structure—no boss, no managers, no bullshit.

The FRIENDS OF AK program is a way you can directly contribute to the continued existence of AK Press, and ensure that we're able to keep publishing books like this one! FRIENDS pay $25 a month directly into our publishing account ($30 for Canada, $35 for international), and receive a copy of every book AK Press publishes for the duration of their membership! Friends also receive a discount on anything they order from our website or buy at a table: 50% on AK titles, and 20% on everything else. We have a FRIENDS OF AK ebook program as well: $15 a month gets you an electronic copy of every book we publish for the duration of your membership. You can even sponsor a very discounted membership for someone in prison.

Email friendsofak@akpress.org for more info, or visit the FRIENDS OF AK PRESS website: https://www.akpress.org/friends.html.

There are always great book projects in the works—so sign up now to become a FRIEND OF AK PRESS, and let the presses roll!